YOU CAN WIN AT LIFE!

You Can Win At Life!

STEVE REDGRAVE AND NICK TOWNSEND

author biographies

Steve Redgrave has enjoyed a rowing career spanning over 25 years and gained a place in the record books for winning gold medals at five Olympic Games in succession. In 2001, the year he was knighted for his sporting achievements, he established the Steve Redgrave Trust, an independent national charity devoted to improving opportunities for children and young people in their local communities. Today his business interests include giving motivational talks to a variety of audiences. He also provides expert analysis for BBC TV's rowing coverage.

Steve is married to Ann, an orthopaedic physician and former international rower, who was team doctor to the Great Britain rowing squad. They have two daughters, Natalie and Sophie, and a son, Zak.

His previous books are *Steven Redgrave's Complete Book of Rowing* (Transworld) and his autobiography, *A Golden Age* (BBC Books).

Nick Townsend is Chief Sports Writer for the *Independent on Sunday*, and was previously a sports writer for the *Daily Mail*. This book is his second collaboration with Steve Redgrave, his first being Steve's autobiography. He lives in Oxfordshire with his wife, Louise.

First published 2005
Copyright © Sir Steve Redgrave and Nick Townsend 2005
The moral right of the author has been asserted.

All rights reserved. No part of this book may be reproduced in any form or by any means without prior written permission from the publisher, except by a reviewer who may quote brief passages in a review.

ISBN 0 563 48776 3

Published by BBC Books, BBC Worldwide Ltd, Woodlands, 80 Wood Lane, London W12 0TT

Commissioning editor: Ben Dunn and Nicky Ross
Project editors: Sarah Sutton and Laura Nickoll
Copy-editors: Tessa Clark and Patricia Burgess
Designer: Isobel Gillan/Ben Cracknell Studios
Production controller: Kenneth McKay

Printed and bound in Great Britain by CPI Bath

Contents

introduction   8

CHAPTER 1
identify your dreams   16

CHAPTER 2
what is your potential?   35

CHAPTER 3
plan to succeed   51

CHAPTER 4
be flexible and use stepping-stones   71

CHAPTER 5
look ahead and stay ahead   98

CHAPTER 6
train to win   117

CHAPTER 7
learn from the experts   134

CHAPTER 8
establish a mental edge   149

CHAPTER 9
leadership and working within a team   168

CHAPTER 10
enjoying success and facing the future   182

timeline   188

Redgrave's reminders   190

introduction

REDGRAVE'S RULE:

❝ WINNING IS NOT JUST ABOUT CROSSING THE LINE FIRST. ❞

For over 25 years I was one of Britain's elite athletes. Throughout my career, and even more so since I retired in 2000, people in all walks of life, many of them involved with sport, but also business people, have asked me: 'How can I, too, be a winner? What is your winning formula?'

I tell them right at the outset that winning involves not just one factor. It is a question of improving every aspect of their lives.

Certainly, not everyone can become an Olympic champion. Nor can every entrepreneur or business person become a millionaire. It is also unlikely that someone who can't boil an egg will be transformed into a master chef overnight. Just as there is no elixir for prolonging life, and no formula for converting base metals into gold, I cannot pretend that I possess the wizardry to change people's lives with the wave of a magic wand. But I believe that my experiences, and what I have gained from them, can help everyone get more out of their lives.

Many people might be tempted to ask: 'What can a sportsman teach business people? He's talking about the elite end of sport. How can a rower advise someone in a boardroom or on the shop floor? What can a man like Redgrave tell me? He excelled at a certain sport. He had the physical prowess and determination to succeed, but maybe he just got lucky. What can he teach the rest of us about improving our lives?'

Well, it's true that the closest I have come to being in a 'normal' working environment was delivering leaflets advertising my local newspaper when I was a teenager. But in many ways putting together a series of crews is similar to managing a team in the workplace, and rowing in a winning crew requires the kind of determination and dedication that will ensure success in almost any walk of life.

In my view, the lessons we learn from sport can be applied to many aspects of life, whether preparing for the Olympics, running a business or concentrating on getting a university degree. They can apply to everything: sport, work, life in general. I'm not talking about techniques. This is not about blades in the water or accuracy with a football. It's about motivating yourself to achieve the best.

Rowing, once considered one of the great amateur sports, is now run on a highly professional basis. It is meticulously structured, and thus provides an exemplar for many of the ideas I try to get across. Certainly, when giving motivational speeches at companies throughout the United Kingdom and beyond, I receive highly positive reactions – otherwise I wouldn't be invited back. No doubt I was initially asked to speak primarily because I was in the media eye after Sydney 2000, and they thought a five-times Olympic gold medallist would be a great motivator.

I'm proud to be recognized for achieving what I have in sport. It's nice that people ask me to give presentations. I really enjoy that. But I don't crave adulation. When I talk, I believe strongly in

introduction

what I'm trying to put across. I believe that, because of what I've achieved, I have a unique perspective. I hope I can help everyone, be they elite or amateur sports people, business executives, or those who are simply striving to get more out of life, by sharing my knowledge.

Many books of this kind tend to be based on theory. However, I use my own personal experiences and those of people with whom I've trained and worked. Wherever possible, I give real examples from my own career and the careers of people I have known.

Insurance companies have featured a lot among the institutions that have invited me to talk. Insurance is an industry that tends to have a high staff turnover, so I often find that I am talking to people who've been in my audience before – but when they were working for another company. I've been gratified when some of them come up to me and say: 'I heard you speak before and you made me think about how I structure myself and how I do things.' I touch on many different areas in my speeches, and I have found that different elements have different effects on different people. That's why I don't emphasize any particular area. I talk about the big picture.

This book was inspired by the reactions I get when I talk to sportsmen and women and to business audiences. One question that often gets thrown at me is: 'Now you are going into business yourself, are you structuring things the same way as you did in sport?' That's always a difficult one to answer. In theory: yes, I am. In practice: well, I'm getting there.

This book is about how you, too, can get where you want to go. Within these pages I frequently use the dreams I myself have realized as examples of what can be achieved in life. After more than 25 years in rowing, this is the area I know best. But where possible, I have included other examples to take you through the stages that will enable you to win at life:

- Visualizing and defining your dreams and desires
- Recognizing your potential
- Setting your goals
- Planning how to achieve your goals
- Training your body and mind
- Staying ahead
- Leading or being a member of a team

PLANNING AHEAD

One of my business interests is a leisure-clothing brand, Five Gold. Established following the Sydney Olympics, it was a simple enough concept at the time, and an obvious one in the circumstances. Now I have to think: 'Where do we want to be in ten years' time? What share of the market do we want to have?' Every so often, I have to ask my colleagues: 'Where do you see us in two or five years' time?' I try to get them to think the way I used to think when I was rowing.

It wouldn't be right for me to give motivational speeches to other companies if I couldn't make a success of my own business ventures.

When I talk of winning I use the word in its broadest sense. Everyone can improve on what they do. Winning for most people means a series of personal victories. It's not just about ability. It's about preparing correctly and doing things methodically. Excelling at sport isn't about running lots of miles and pulling lots of weights. Success in business is not about flogging yourself to the point of exhaustion, and achieving the lifestyle you want doesn't mean that you first have to win the Lottery.

Success can be measured in many ways. For me, securing five gold medals was the ultimate success: my way of measuring myself against the world. But success can also be finishing a marathon five minutes faster than you trained for, even if your placing is 56th. It can be getting a higher pay rise than you asked for, or losing just a few ounces more weight than you expected to lose.

Whenever you are prone to self-doubt, whenever you are tempted to shrug and say, 'I just haven't got it' or 'So and so's always had far more ability than me', tell yourself this simple truth: 'People more talented than me have achieved less.'

Whatever the context, remember that winning isn't necessarily about beating opponents. It can also mean getting to the finish line of a challenge you have set yourself.

learning to win

No one should expect that merely by analysing themselves and their ambitions they will achieve the changes they seek to make in their lives. Learning to be a winner will be tough going, and there will be times when you will be tempted to stray from your path.

I understand that. To reach where I am today I have had to overcome some very low points. How I have realized my dreams, and the ways in which other people should attempt to do the same, forms the basis of my speeches. The purpose of this book is to look at these ideas and see how you can apply them, whether you are a young sportsman or woman, a budding entrepreneur, or simply someone who wants to realize their unfulfilled potential.

The results of success and failure are very obvious within sport. Among teams the sense of failure is usually quite short-lived because they will already be thinking ahead, probably in positive terms, to the next match. In this case, failure tends not to reflect on one individual – the team shares the responsibility. The same usually holds true in business and the workplace.

When you're on your own, however, failure and setbacks have to be dealt with as swiftly and positively as possible. We've all had bad experiences. The best way of coping is not to close your mind to what went wrong, but to work through it in your head and use what you learn from it to strengthen you for the future.

Olympic sports are judged on one victory once every four years. If you come tenth in the 100 metres, you are thought of – harshly, I should add – as a failure. You're nobody. Contrast this with commerce. If you come tenth in the list of the world's most successful businessmen, people will look up to you and talk about the amazing empire you have created. Or take pop music: in that industry, if you have a number one hit, you're recognized as being

introduction

successful. If you have several, you're extremely successful. But there are potentially 52 hits each year. Even at number two, you're a success. I've been heavily involved in the 2012 London Olympic bid. As with the Games themselves, there is a winning line, and there will be only one winner. The rest will be losers.

Athletes today have help from many sources, not just coaches. Any successful young sportsman or woman has advisers, coaches, sports psychologists and mentors. Rightly so. Before the 2004 Olympics I was asked to pass on my experience to six young athletes with Olympic potential under the Team Visa scheme. I advised them on a variety of areas relating to their preparation for Athens, and was pleased to help.

I started out as nothing more than a schoolboy with potential. I did not attend a traditional rowing school or university. Unlike youngsters today who display a talent for the sport, I had no guidance, no one to lead me up the mountain of my aspirations. My coach and I, and the crews I rowed in, had to find the way to achieve by ourselves. We made mistakes and learnt lessons along the way. Now I devote much of my time passing on my experiences.

In this book I look back on my career and what I have assimilated from both a physical and a mental standpoint. I have learnt by watching and listening to others, and I have also been inspired by others – not least, the swimmer Mark Spitz, who won seven Olympic gold medals in one Olympic Games in 1972. I hope that I too can be an inspiration.

By the mere act of purchasing this book you have demonstrated that you want to better yourself. Or, at the very least, that you are questioning your present lifestyle, asking questions such as: 'How can I detect and reveal my unrealized potential?' I hope that what you read may prompt you to challenge the way you live. If it doesn't – if you say, 'Well, I'm quite happy with what I'm doing. This is how I want to live my life' – that's fine. But there will, I hope, be at least some element in the book that inspires you to re-evaluate your situation.

For some time I have wanted to put my ideas down on paper and introduce them to a wider audience. I feel now is the right time.

Good luck in your quest to be a winner.

Sir Steve Redgrave
January 2005

CHAPTER 1

identify your dreams

> REDGRAVE'S RULE:
>
> **' THINK THE UNTHINKABLE. '**

Dreams are the essence of this book. Not in the sense of idle, fanciful imaginings, or the ones you have during sleep, but as aspirations you desire to realize. Before you can do this, however, you need to identify your dreams and decide which ones are achievable.

an olympian vision

A few years ago, my wife Ann and I were asked to speak about our rowing careers to a group of young rowers at Hampton School in Molesey, southwest London. Although I agreed, I can't say I was enthralled by the prospect. My initial thought was: 'How the hell am I going to go about this?' How could I explain the desires and inspiration that were the genesis of a career that lasted over 25 years?

However, this got me thinking about the whole process of turning ambition into reality, and when, a little later, I was invited to give another speech – at the Leander Club in Henley, where I used to train as an international oarsman – I talked about The Dream. I told my audience that not everyone can be an Olympic champion. Similarly, not everyone can be the top student or most successful businessman. But everyone can perform better if they plan and structure their life correctly. This is the central theme of this book.

The Dream can mean many things. It may mean retiring to a villa in an area of Spain you love. Perhaps it will mean acquiring a job or position you've always coveted. For younger readers, it may represent playing for the football team they've always supported. It needn't necessarily involve just you as a solitary individual. That hunger for success can be satisfied by achievement in a team environment, on the sporting field or in the workplace.

never look back with regret

Whatever your dream, you must have a Vision of success. A Challenge. A Target. Never look back with regret and think of 'what might have been' later in life merely because you didn't recognize your dream and plot your future accordingly.

Though it is true that I stumbled into a sport for which I discovered I had a talent, my imagination had already been fired when I thrilled to the spectacle on television of the prolific American swimmer Mark Spitz at the 1972 Olympic Games. Spitz won seven gold medals, each in a world record time. Even the remarkable 'Thorpedo', Ian Thorpe, Australia's modern-day equivalent, or the USA's Michael Phelps, cannot compare with that. As a ten-year-old, I thought it was pretty fantastic. I said to myself: 'Seven Olympic gold medals. I'd like to win one at something. That's got to be brilliant.'

identify your dreams

I wanted to emulate Mark Spitz, though not necessarily in swimming. Like any child, I had other dreams, too. I also used to imagine myself walking out at Wembley and then scoring a winning goal in an FA Cup final. I haven't given up that dream. It just hasn't come true!

Even then, I was consumed with the thought of winning; not just taking part. But, most importantly, I had an ambition, something to inspire me. It was to win an Olympic gold medal – even though at that stage I had no idea that it would be for rowing.

We all have dreams as children. Today, many youngsters believe they can be another David Beckham, Michael Owen, Wayne Rooney, or maybe Jonny Wilkinson. Others will be inspired by watching Tim Henman or Wimbledon champion Roger Federer, or perhaps golfer Tiger Woods. Some may dream they will one day become television presenters or pop singers.

As we get older, most of our dreams become more modest and, almost certainly, achievable. But there are also the significant ones that lie dormant, probably suppressed by the belief that 'This is the wrong time' or 'I'm not good enough' or any of the many other excuses we invent for ourselves. They are dreams waiting to be awoken. This is their time.

In order to progress, it is vital to keep reminding yourself that you can achieve, rather than search for reasons why you cannot. There are people who, for all manner of reasons – but most frequently on the grounds of your age – will attempt to deflate your ambitions. Just don't let these 'dream-stealers' (as Monty Roberts, better known as the 'horse whisperer', describes them) deflect you from your path. You're never too old. If at 50 you are determined to run your first marathon, and your friends say you're past it or you're not fit enough, don't be deterred. Just completing the course will make you a winner.

DREAM-STEALERS

- You're too unfit to trek in the Himalayas.
- You're too extravagant to save a deposit for a house or flat.
- You're too short to be a model.
- You're too tall to be a ballet dancer.
- You don't have the willpower to lose weight.
- You don't have what it takes to be a team leader.
- You don't work well with other members of a team.

identify your dreams

The first step towards life change is list your ambitions and aspirations. This can seem daunting. It's probably how novelists feel when they begin their work. The clue is to write down *something*, however far-fetched or outlandish, and other ideas will take root from this. Allow your imagination to run riot. Think of your mind as a butterfly net, and sweep every possible thought into it, no matter how exotic it may seem.

identify your dreams

It's important to consider all possibilities, including ones you may have previously rejected because you thought: 'I couldn't possibly achieve that' or 'My current lifestyle couldn't accommodate that'. Try compiling a wish list of 20 dreams on all manner of subjects: your income, house, job, recreation, health and fitness.... If you have always harboured the ambition to run a bed and breakfast in Devon, or a ski chalet in Austria, say so. Just write down what really excites you, no matter how crazy it may sound. Some dreams may be short term – losing weight, for example. Others may change your life more radically. But don't worry – you will have the opportunity to prioritize and refine them all later.

As I told the students at Hampton School: 'The alternative is simply to leave things to chance, to fate, as many people do. Do that, and you may get lucky, but it's more likely that you won't.'

An excellent example of a sportsman who started out with a dream was Great Britain track cyclist Bradley Wiggins, who at the age of 24 became the triple Olympic medallist in 2004. I was present when he took gold in the individual pursuit event at the velodrome in Athens. He also won silver and bronze in two other events, making him the most successful British Olympian at a single Games since Mary Rand in 1964. He talks about his dream: 'Since I was a boy, I've never lived beyond 24,' he says. 'This was always my life's goal, winning Olympic gold. I've never really had disappointments on the way, like, say, Kelly Holmes with all her injuries. I've been very lucky. I've never really had too many setbacks. My life's been a series of progressions every year.'

Bradley was initially inspired – as I had been – by an Olympic performance. He began cycling in 1992 after watching Chris

Boardman win a gold medal in Barcelona. Within five years, he had progressed to win the world junior pursuit title, and a year later earned a Commonwealth team pursuit silver. At Sydney in 2000, Bradley secured an Olympic team pursuit bronze. His career developed steadily, and in 2003 he claimed a world pursuit gold medal. However, his eye was always on the big prize, just as mine had been in rowing: 'I was only 20 when I won a bronze in Sydney in the team pursuit,' he says. 'Of course, I enjoyed that, but I just thought to myself: "Right, I'll get a gold next time."'

As the Great Britain cycling performance director Dave Brailsford said after Athens: 'Bradley's a very focused and driven individual, as most Olympic champions are. He's dreamed of this for 12 years, and has worked to make that dream a reality. He's looked at every aspect of his sport to achieve that.'

Bradley speaks of luck, and everyone successful needs that. But he also showed focus in pursuing his goal. He planned ahead and had the determination and tenacity to stick to his strategy. All these are important elements in winning at life.

it's always the day for a daydream…

We all daydream at some stage, and I believe it's an important part of life. As schoolchildren we've all allowed our attention to wander during a tedious lesson. This is, understandably, discouraged by teachers. Yet daydreaming has an important role to play in our development.

Sports psychologists say that, for an athlete, daydreaming is very much a positive rather than a negative. Why should this not be true in other walks of life, too?

visualize your dreams

Daydreaming, in the sense that it is a time you set aside for allowing your mind to mull over a whole range of ideas, is actually a form of visualization – creating vivid mind pictures – a practice that I believe is crucial when preparing for sport. As described in Chapter 5, I used visualization in my rowing career as a means of mental rehearsal for forthcoming major events. But it can be applied to all manner of circumstances, from closing a business deal to preparing for an interview. It has even been used by pregnant women to help them relax before the birth. All those who use visualization find it helps to release tension and stress. It provides, if you like, an inner space in which to relax the mind and body.

There are roughly 8 million pieces of information entering your brain at any one time. What visualization does is to filter everything so that your mind concentrates only on the important bits.

Whatever your dream – the career you crave, the life change you covet, the weight loss you desire – visualize it and write down every thought it provokes. How good does it make you feel?

> **EXERCISE:** ANYONE CAN VISUALIZE
>
> Give yourself at least 20 minutes in a place where you won't be disturbed by phone, family or friends. Sit comfortably, then close your eyes and picture in your mind something that you'd like to attain – perhaps your ideal house. Never mind for the moment that it may be beyond you financially. What does it look like? What are the rooms like? What kind of style is it? What is the view? What kind of garden does it have? What are the colours, the smells? You could even think about what emotions it evokes. Imagine you and your family living there.
>   That, in essence, is visualization: a mental picture of your dream realized.

If weight loss is your goal, picture yourself not just as a vague entity, but as a vivid colourful image of your slimmer self. How are people reacting to the new you? Do you feel more confident?

Once a day, maybe twice, go through the feelings you have written down and visualize the person you aim to become.

give yourself time to think

The need to make time to think may seem obvious, but too many people ignore the good sense of this. They race breathlessly through the day, performing tasks almost instinctively, and then sit back and

identify your dreams

think: 'Now, have I done that correctly?' and 'Have I forgotten anything?' We run into problems because we don't pause and think.

Many business leaders lock themselves in their offices, away from other people and their opinions, to consider their long-term strategies. They contemplate the larger picture. Top bosses have obviously to be aware of problems that arise in their offices and factories, of the nitty-gritty that has to be addressed, but they also know they mustn't take their eye off the main ball and the overall goal that see their company is working towards.

This makes a lot of sense, and it applies equally in normal life. If taking time off to focus on the bigger picture is not something you do, isn't it time you changed? Think about it for a moment. Concentrating on the problems of everyday life means that the big picture is obscured. Don't allow yourself to be overwhelmed by detail. Instead, focus on the big picture – your Dream, Vision or Challenge – and you will find that this drives the detail.

When I was preparing to take part in the London Marathon in 2001, the year after the Sydney Olympics, I found it useful to think while I was out running. I wanted to take my mind off the training, and it was a way of putting my life in perspective. I was able to consider what was important and what I needed to focus on. I did this while I was running, but you could do this in the bath, while listening to music, or driving to and from work. Keep a notebook by the side of your bed and jot down any thoughts that come to you when you wake up. If you feel that physical exercise will help spark inspiration, try dancing to your favourite music – or just take a quick walk around the block.

Whether you are evaluating your long-term plans, or merely contemplating the next few days, it is vital that you make time to think in order to have a clear vision of where you want to be at a prescribed time.

Albert Einstein understood this. He used to sit and contemplate life in a special 'thinking chair' – and he probably required such an aid rather less than the rest of us! It was Einstein who said: 'Imagination is everything. It is the preview of life's coming attractions.' That is well worth remembering.

define your dreams

Earlier, I asked you to write a wish list of your dreams, no matter how fanciful they were. This is always a useful exercise. It allows your imagination to run wild; you can consider every possibility. Now comes the difficult part: deciding which dreams are realistic and manageable.

This doesn't mean limiting yourself unnecessarily. Maybe some of your aspirations can be put on hold for the time being. What it does mean is taking a rational approach and condensing everything down to what can be achieved with the talents you have, or – and this is important – the talents you could have. Of course, before you start to acquire new abilities, your first consideration should be to concentrate on, and develop, the ones you have.

To explain many of the concepts in this book, I frequently refer to the Olympics. I do so not only because it is an area with which

identify your dreams

I am familiar, but because the Games demand a variety of strengths. In this way preparing for them is not dissimilar to the needs of the business world. Indeed, they reflect life in general.

Just as you don't become an Olympic champion in days, you won't become a millionaire overnight – short of buying a winning lottery ticket. This doesn't rule out achieving these dreams, provided you have the latent ability and determination. But in general it is preferable to have more modest goals and succeed at them, rather than fail with a project that is ridiculously overambitious.

A dream may be long term or short term. It all depends on the context. If you're an elite athlete, the dream will almost certainly be the next Olympics. That is a focused point in the future, four years on from the last Games. Similarly, if your dream is to complete a half-marathon, your mind will be fixed on a certain date, maybe a year or two years ahead. In the short term, you might want to start on a keep-fit campaign.

In business there are many different areas in which you can define your ultimate dream. Monthly and annual targets are all-important, but you may also have to take into account the progress of your company 10, 15, even 20 years ahead. You may have to re-evaluate your dream as the years pass.

In general, I'd suggest that your dreams should be restricted to ones where you can see a definite result in the short term. If you look too far ahead, results tend to become vague. Return to your wish list of dreams, and decide which of them are achievable in the not-too-distant future. Then you can progress to the next stages – recognizing your potential and planning a strategy for success.

dreams come in many shapes and forms

If your dream is to lose weight, to be fitter, to be in better shape, to be healthier, it is as valid as wanting to create a new life for yourself and family. However, just thinking vaguely about it will achieve little. In Chapter 3 I tell you how you can set your goals and make them achievable. With this in mind, it's time to refine your dreams.

Imagine now that your mind is giant strainer, a mental version of the kitchen utensil, if you like. You want to retain the 'goodness' in your dreams and dispense with the residue. To do this your assessments will have to be harsh, but, as I constantly stress, this doesn't mean you shouldn't be adventurous in your thinking. Let's look at an example.

CASE STUDY

Colin and Christine *(mid-forties)*

Like many people nowadays, Colin and his wife Christine, parents of two teenage boys, are intoxicated by the concept of buying a house, villa or small chateau abroad. Their dream is to refurbish it and run it as a B&B or hotel, but they fear the cost would be prohibitive. Would it? Have they done any research? Have they actually investigated the financial implications? They also have to consider how they would cope with a foreign language and the legal implications of living in another country. And, for that matter, how good are their culinary skills?

> But the crucial question they must answer is this: do they truly wish to escape the rat race in Britain, or would such a radical change of environment be alien to them and their family? Do they have the potential to succeed or are they inherently frightened of the unknown? (Potential is discussed more fully in Chapter 2.)
>
> As Colin and Christine are approaching middle age, they must also ask if they have the energy and focus for such an upheaval. And what would the effect be on their relationship and that with their children?
>
> If the couple have been harbouring this dream for a long time but have done nothing about it – not even a quick browse through properties on the Internet – it suggests that they are not really serious: we all have pipe dreams. But if they genuinely want to pursue the idea further, they must think clearly about all the factors described above, and employ a degree of visualization (see Chapter 5) before making a decision.

These are the kinds of question that need to be asked when you set about realizing your dreams; and this book will take you, step by step, through all these stages.

your boundaries can be limitless

No one can run 100 metres in zero seconds. Well, of course they can't. There will always be a limit, a boundary of some kind, to what can be achieved. But this shouldn't preclude us from attempting to improve on what has been done before.

How fast will we ultimately be able to run? Mathematicians and physiologists might say that if everything is at an optimum, an athlete would be able to achieve 100 metres in 5.6 seconds. But who knows how the human physique will change? I remember that when I was 13 and already over 1.80 metres (6 feet) tall, I was told that I was taller than most adult ancient Romans. If I'd been around at the time of the Roman Empire, I'd have been considered a freak!

Over the years, as human beings evolve, it is likely that times to complete distances will continue to decrease. Nevertheless, unless the design of *Homo sapiens* alters in some remarkable way, maybe because of climate change, and we develop the speed of a cheetah, there will always be a physical limitation to how fast humans can run. What that boundary will be, we simply don't know.

Yet it is in our nature to push ourselves to our limits, to break records and create new personal bests. How else do we explain the continued popularity of *The Guinness Book of Records* – from the perspective of both readers and potential entrants?

World records will continue to be set and, like Bob Beamon's long jump record, could stand for many years. The American athlete's leap of 8.90 metres (29.2 feet) at the 1968 Mexico City Olympics broke the previous record by a remarkable 60 cm (2 feet). Although it was inevitable that somebody would eventually beat Beamon's distance, what was astonishing was that his record lasted 23 years – until 1991.

identify your dreams

Other records, however, are broken remarkably quickly. Looking back some 20 years, I remember our coxed four crew lowering the world record at Lucerne in the build-up to my first Olympics, in Los Angeles in 1984, after which we became favourites to win. We beat the East Germans. We came off the water and everybody declared that our time would never be beaten; that it would stand for years. In fact, it was beaten within 24 hours! The East Germans did it when they raced the following day and we decided not to take part. Conditions had been good for us, but were even better for our rivals.

When the current Great Britain rowing coach, Jurgen Grobler, came to Britain from Germany in the early 1990s he set us a 'gold' time. This was the target he calculated we had to reach to win a gold medal at the next Olympics. The time set was 6 minutes 22 seconds (6.22) to cover the standard 2000 metres in the coxless pairs. Everyone said: 'People can't go that fast. That's just ridiculous compared with what everybody's done before.'

Yet Andy Holmes and I had done 6.24 in training. Andy was my first Olympic partner, with whom I won gold in the coxed four at Los Angeles in 1984 and in the pairs at Seoul four years later. In the right conditions in a race environment, assuming the weather was in our favour, I knew we'd probably be able to go that much quicker and find two seconds.

As it turned out, Matthew Pinsent and I broke the world record in Indianapolis in 1994. Matthew was my partner in the gold-medal-winning coxless pairs at the 1992 and 1996 Olympics, and member of the victorious Sydney 2000 four. Our record stood for eight years.

Currently, the world record for the pairs is 6.14. Now there is talk about a record of 6.10 being set, which is pretty damn quick – certainly unthinkable when I set out on my career. I wouldn't have been capable of doing that, or 6.14. But some competitors will achieve it. One day.

What can we learn from this example? Principally that we should not allow ourselves to be deterred by the self-defeating limits we place on ourselves. It is always easy to find excuses for not achieving something – perhaps even for not attempting it in the first place.

Reflect back on occasions in any context – school, university or work – when you have settled for second best or even worse. Have you allowed yourself to think, 'I couldn't possibly cope' or 'That's beyond me', but in hindsight recognized that thinking that way was just taking the easy way out?

Perhaps somebody has been promoted above you at work. Never mind that you were the better qualified for promotion, it was self-publicist Richard who was propelled up the greasy pole. You rationalize it by saying to yourself: 'Well, I suppose Richard had the personality for that promotion. Perhaps I didn't. Oh, and I didn't really want it anyway – it involved too much responsibility. Let Richard take the flack when the heat's on and the team's not working effectively.'

Now try to be brutally honest with yourself. Think through that situation as though you are an outside observer without any preconceptions. Don't dwell on the actions of any other people who may have been involved. Just consider your own.

> **EXERCISE:** LEARN FROM SELF-LIMITING BEHAVIOUR
>
> - Use hindsight to decide how you could have handled yourself better in a particular situation. In the case of a failed promotion, did you prepare your case to the management carefully enough and promote your qualities? Did you present it with a confident, positive approach that would have convinced them you were worthy of promotion next time, if not this?
> - Can you honestly say that you did yourself justice? If you didn't, turn the negative experience into a positive one by thinking: 'I could have achieved that if I'd really approached it correctly. Next time I will.'

That analysis, of course, can be applied to any situation, not just in the workplace. It is worth remembering for future reference because there will undoubtedly come another time when you will be faced with a similar situation. Maybe, if you're having doubts about your dreams, you could use it right now.

being realistic needn't limit your horizons

The human frame, and the brain that controls it, is designed with a great deal of 'stretchability'. Physically, mentally and emotionally, we are capable of achievements that we have never even considered. Never forget that as you reflect on your future.

Practise thinking one step ahead of what you think you can do. If you believe that swimming three laps in the pool is the most you can achieve, imagine your satisfaction when you do four. If you think you've reached your maximum earning capacity, visualize what you could do with another £1000 a year.

So where have we arrived? I hope you have expressed your dreams and condensed them so that they are manageable. This balance is important. The toughest part of realizing dreams is making sure that they are not too easy to achieve – but not downright impossible. Take the following example.

A woman who is 1.67 metres (5 feet 7 inches) tall and weighs 76 kg (12 stone) is determined to lose weight. She might yearn for the willowy shape of a Kate Moss, but would have to shed 25 kg (4 stone) – a third of her body weight – to do so. Even getting down to Kate Winslet's 57 kg (9 stone) would be pretty tough going. Far better that she aims to get down to, say, 63 kg (10 stone), and achieves that in gradual stages.

Like this dieter, you can have big dreams, but by this stage you should be analysing them closely and setting challenges that might be tough, sometimes exceedingly tough, but that are achievable. For example, the person who decides to become a barrister late in life might harbour ambitions of becoming a judge, but must acknowledge that the chances of doing so are slim – not impossible, merely improbable.

identify your dreams

Don't let the grandeur of your ultimate ambition deter you from taking steps towards it, and don't let perceptions of yourself (yours or others') limit what you try to do. Who'd have thought, even as recently as a generation ago, that men and women would be sailing single-handed around the world and ascending into the stratosphere in balloons?

Redgrave's reminders

- ✔ Identify your dreams – think as big and bold as you like.
- ✔ Let your mind wander and think the unthinkable. Be adventurous.
- ✔ Take time off to focus on your dreams.
- ✔ Face reality and consider the implications of your dreams.
- ✔ Make your dreams manageable – but don't limit yourself.

CHAPTER 2

what is your potential?

REDGRAVE'S RULE:

❛ BE TRUE TO YOURSELF. ❜

It's human nature to delude ourselves about our true talents. But this is the moment for candour – the time to identify who you really are, not who you imagine yourself to be. Before making any radical changes to your life, you need to evaluate yourself as honestly as possible.

Let's take as an example our gold-medal-winning crew at Sydney: Tim Foster, James Cracknell, Matthew Pinsent and myself – four men in a boat, but each blessed with different talents that complemented those of the others.

Let's look particularly at Tim Foster. He would never possess the strength of other members of the crew but his contribution as a technically proficient oarsman was crucial to our triumph. His laid-back character was very different from that of, say, James Cracknell. James took everything very seriously. But the personalities of these two men complemented each other. Tim recognized his strengths and we appreciated them.

What all of us had in common was that, for all our different temperaments and characters, we were team players. Some people flourish in this environment. Others display their virtues best as solo performers. Some are natural leaders. Others perform to their optimum as members of a team, captained by a charismatic leader.

what is your potential?

Which defines you?

The purpose of this chapter is to show you how to pinpoint and utilize your strengths and improve on your weaker areas.

what kind of person are you?

To set you on your way, I have analysed the reasons for my success as a rower, and identified the factors that made me a champion.

- **physical prowess**
  build
  power
  endurance
  suitability (to the sport)

- **mental strength**
  ability to focus
  ability to adapt,
   to change course

- **technical ability**
  having the basic skills to
   perform at a high level

- **ability to accept advice**
  listening to the coach

- **ability to be a team player**
  being able to do my own
   job effectively
  enhancing the crew
  helping the team to
   improve

- **determination**
  discipline
  routine
  drive
  a will to win

Your task right now is to decide which of your realizable dreams you most wish to achieve and to write down the characteristics you will need to do this. Don't worry if you find you are lacking in some of them. My aim is to help you apply the qualities you do have to your own life, and to inspire you to strengthen your weaknesses.

my story

As a youngster I was a keen athlete, and there was a great tradition of marathon running in Britain. I could have performed creditably enough as a runner, I know that. But this is where realism kicked in at an early age.

I had the physique to win an Olympic gold medal, but at over 107 kg (17 stone) I wasn't going to win it in the marathon. That wasn't realistic. You can't do the impossible and that would have been pretty close to impossible! The heaviest winner of an Olympic marathon wouldn't be much more than half my size. But what is appealing about the Games is that there are so many events. They all require different physical make-ups. Some, such as the marathon, call for extremes of physical endurance; others, such as sprints, require sheer speed; rowing involves a mixture of both, while shooting requires a keen eye and steady hand.

I was a pretty good sprinter as a young boy. I used to win interschool events easily. Unfortunately, my progress was impeded when, for a couple of years, I attended a school where there was a policy of non-competitive sport. I later moved on to the local comprehensive, in Great Marlow in Buckinghamshire, and took up competitive sports again. I was the best sprinter there, but when we competed against other schools on district sports days I found I'd fallen behind and was not in the league I had been in before my non-competitive days. I was being beaten by boys who had previously finished behind me. Was this because I had been out of competitive sport for a time? Or was it because my physical make-up had changed? Had I put on a bit more bulk that slowed me down? It's difficult to say.

The experience taught me a valuable lesson – that we can't all be 'best' at everything all the time. And also that coming second – or even third, fourth or fifth – at something doesn't mean we're not winning at life. There is always an alternative goal.

Fortunately, I soon discovered that my physical make-up gave me the assets to move a boat quite well. I stumbled across this fact accidentally; fortunately today there are initiatives that encourage youngsters who are ideally suited for certain sports, such as rowing. In the past, people became rowers if they went to a certain school or university. I went to neither; just an ordinary comprehensive. Luck had it that one of the teachers, Francis Smith, took a particular interest in rowing, and he soon realized that the elements it demanded suited my physique.

Five Olympic gold medals resulted from my going out in a boat during school time – something that I regarded as a good 'skive'.

EXERCISE: NOW IT'S YOUR TURN...

Using the analysis of my own characteristics on page 36 as a guide, list in two columns your strengths and weaknesses. In the weakness column, underline the areas where you believe you may have potential. This is important.

You may be aware, for instance, that you currently have a lack of qualifications or experience to carry out a particular job. That doesn't mean you shouldn't gain them if you have sufficient desire to do so. These days there are thousands of courses – full time, part time, evening classes, home study, you name it – from which you can gain qualifications and experience. If you are enthusiastic about starting your own business, a course in basic accountancy would clearly be invaluable if figures aren't one of your strong points.

decide what motivates you

As well as identifying the kind of person you are, you need to evaluate what it is that motivates you. The exercise below will help you to consider what is important to you. It will also enable you to identify what really drives you and makes you tick, and the kind of life you really desire. It may take time. You may change your mind after an initial assessment, but however long it takes, be honest.

Don't give answers that simply make you feel good. You will only cheat yourself. And remember: being a winner is not necessarily about material wealth, or finishing highest on the podium. It is about achieving what you set out to do; it is about crossing your own line first, no matter how grand or how modest your ambitions may be.

> **EXERCISE:** WHAT MOTIVATES YOU?
>
> Pick five of the following aspirational phrases that best sum up your priorities:
> - Becoming a millionaire
> - Making good money
> - Making very good money
> - Enjoying the freedom and absence of stress in a less-demanding occupation, but that doesn't necessarily pay well
> - Improving my career
> - Running my own business
> - Enhancing my status in the community
> - Living in the location of my choice
> - Enjoying a stimulating and harmonious family life
> - Indulging myself in my pastime or sport
> - Making a contribution to the community, perhaps through charity work

A lot of people will be motivated by most, or many, of the aspirations in the exercise. However, it is important that you prioritize what inspires you because inevitably there will be conflicts. Some of your choices may be mutually exclusive: a successful career is not always compatible with a balanced family life; an interesting career may not equate with accumulating significant wealth; a successful career may mean relocating to a place where you'd rather not live, and so on. Knowing your personal preferences and those of the people around you is important. If you are going to achieve your full potential in life, it is vital that those important to you share your goals.

how ambitious are you?

Ambitious people talk about having a fire in their belly. I call it determination. Most people, I suspect, work because they want the money that allows them to pay the mortgage and provides them with security. Their actual occupation is of less importance. Some, however, work in a job they love for its own sake, regardless of the rewards.

It is important to scrutinize the bigger picture. I hope answering the following questions will assist you in determining how ambitious you are:

- Are you prepared to put in the amount of hard work involved in attempting to become one of the precious few who make it to the top, whether in business or sport?

- To what extent are you prepared to sacrifice security and take on the risks frequently involved with ambition? Remember that sportsmen and women (outside the 'professional' arenas of football, tennis, golf, cricket, rugby and a few others) may have to devote so much energy – not to mention so much of their income – to their particular discipline that everything else in their lives suffers.
- Are you able to see, even though there are no guarantees of success, the benefits of trying outweigh the status quo?
- Are you prepared to accept that if you were to give up your salaried, relatively secure job to become self-employed, with the prospect of greater rewards, you might suffer financially in the initial stages, and perhaps even in the long term?
- Would you be happy with the lifestyle changes you would probably have to make to achieve your dream, and the domestic turmoil that might result?
- Or, in reality, do you crave the security (or as close as you're going to get) of a regular occupation?

These are the kind of questions I've had to ask myself in various forms during the last 25 years. You will have to ask yourself these, and many others, before you begin your progress to becoming a winner.

So, having looked at closely at *who* you are, your *motivational drive* and your *ambition*, one question remains…

are you absolutely sure you want to be a winner?

Well, of course. Why else would you be reading this book? Yet as you daydream and contemplate your future, there will undoubtedly be times when you experience a tinge of self-doubt. It happens to virtually all of us because winning requires facing a personal challenge, or demands taking a risk. Sometimes it involves both.

Weight loss, for example, requires food deprivation and maybe a keep-fit regime. Neither would be happily undertaken by most people because they're almost certain to involve discomfort and pain. Similarly, a career change almost certainly means extra work, and carries a risk that it could all go wrong. Those whom we regard as winners would say that few of the things worth having in life are without risk, but risk remains something that many people would prefer to avoid.

Here, again, visualization is important (see page 23). Try to envisage just how rewarding life could be if you go ahead and take that risky step. Hold on to that image to remind you of the 'promised land' in troubled times during your journey.

Would you be happier remaining Jack or Jill Average? It's inevitable that this thought will go through your mind at some stage. Fear of change and fear of failure are emotions that everyone experiences – when moving house, for example, or looking for a new job. Far better the devil you know, some say.

what is your potential?

are you a risk-taker or a percentage player?

Sport is a useful analogy when you are trying to decide what kind of person you are. Let's consider golf. Any keen player and watcher knows that the professional game tends to be divided between courageous performers who relish taking risks, such as the mercurial Spaniard Sergio Garcia and the sartorially flamboyant Ian Poulter, and percentage players who prefer a safer, more conservative approach, such as Nick Faldo, and Colin Montgomerie in his heyday.

Many experts favour what is called 'percentage' golf, where the player goes for shots that are likely to come off, and wins by making fewer mistakes than his more adventurous rivals. But some players, like Poulter and Garcia, who've got the cavalier spirit in their psyche, don't have it in them to do anything other than take risks. The reality is, of course, that all golfers play to their strengths. If a player's strength is percentage golf, that's the way he plays; if he's a risk-taker, the kind of golfer who goes for shots that even experienced commentators can't see, it makes sense to stick to that approach.

The same applies in other walks of life. What sort of player are you? If you fear failure and any decline in your material and emotional welfare, you are not a risk-taker. You are a percentage player – a person whose policy is safety first. Your natural tendency is to restrict losses to a minimum and aim for the higher percentage – just like a Faldo or Montgomerie.

It's important at this stage that you get to know yourself. That's why you have to identify your strengths and weaknesses. Again, some candour is required. It's as well to look closely at your potential before you embark on a dream that will make new demands on you.

what is your potential?

> **CASE STUDY**
>
> ### Louise (25)
>
> Having been left £200,000 by an elderly relative, Louise has to decide between three alternatives. Should she place the money in a savings account to give her some security if times turn hard in the future? Should she invest all of it in a small company she and a friend have always wanted to set up to exploit their talents as artists? Or should she simply spend it on herself and her family?
>
> Louise's attitude to life is 'live for today, not tomorrow', so she wants gratification now, not at some point in the future. It's no surprise, therefore, that she decides to buy new cars, clothes and holidays for herself and her family rather than using the money for long-term security.

And here's a topical example for you to consider...

> **CASE STUDY**
>
> ### David and Sue (late forties)
>
> Bored by their comfortable but predictable lives, David and Sue are considering going into property development, lured by all those television programmes that give the impression that transforming a shabby shell into a designer abode is a relatively straightforward process. Once this was considered to be the domain of professionals.

> Now renovating properties has become popular with amateur enthusiasts. Yet, as we are all aware, house-buying can be a hazardous business at the best of times.
>
> The couple will be spending many thousands of pounds on a structure that might conceal all manner of horrors. And there's always the niggling thought that the house they're selling to finance their project might unexpectedly acquire extra value and turn into a gold mine.
>
> David and Sue decide to go ahead with their dream, but they've done their homework and their eyes are wide open to the pitfalls of their undertaking. Fired by hope, alert to problems and determined to work hard and succeed, they have all the fundamentals in place to reach their goal.

All these case studies are excellent examples of risks. And in each case the people concerned need to ask whether the radical changes they are considering are right for them. Do they have the character and temperament to make them work? Think about times in your own life when you've had to choose between various options. What did you decide to do? Did you take a risk, or were you a percentage player?

Remember, there is absolutely no point in taking what most people would consider to be highly risky decisions if you're not by nature that kind of person. If you embark on a high-risk route, you must be confident that you could accept a serious knock-back if things didn't entirely go to plan.

Visualization (see page 22) will help. Sit in a room alone, without distractions, and play your vision through your mind as though it was on a DVD. Your thoughts should give you feelings of pleasure. Try introducing your reservations. To what extent do they concern you? Are they insurmountable? Don't press stop until you've examined the disk fully for possible future problems.

Fear of the unknown, of failure, of financial ruin – even of making a fool of yourself – are all natural emotions, and reasons for caution in some circumstances. But they are not reasons for giving up on your dream. If it is worth anything, you will be confronted by obstacles at some time. It's part of life's rougher terrain. Sometimes it's necessary to take a leap of faith.

don't settle for less than you're worth

Whatever your dream, it will undoubtedly demand that you push yourself – maybe harder than ever before. You may have to sail through uncharted waters. This can be an uncomfortable and sometimes hazardous experience but it doesn't mean you are not capable of achieving your aim. It shouldn't provide an excuse for abandoning the whole project.

Most people, when they analyse themselves, realize that they have achieved more than they had imagined. Think about it. On how many occasions have you had a dream, in the most general sense of the word, and achieved what you set out to do? Think back to your schooldays. Did you ever say to yourself, 'Well, I'm not brilliant academically, but I reckon I can gain a certain number of exam passes,' and then done so? On the sports field you may have been pretty good at the high jump. Maybe your sports teacher said: 'Right, there's no reason why you can't clear so many centimetres.' And you did it.

winners are people like you

Gather all the information you can about people who have achieved excellence. Read about them in newspapers and books; watch programmes about them on television. You don't necessarily have to like them! You will find that many entrepreneurs and adventurers come from ordinary, sometimes humble, backgrounds. They will have made mistakes. Some overcame them and bounced back immediately; some took longer. But all developed a faith in themselves.

Consider the explorer Ranulph Fiennes, who in 1996, at the age of 52, and with two much younger companions, stepped into a blizzard towing a 225-kg (500-lb) sledge, ready to brave Antarctica – a total of around 2000 km (1300 miles). He was no fitness fanatic – or wasn't until he prepared for the expedition. As he admits himself, he had smoked on and off for years, was a chocoholic, loved roasts, fries and cream cakes, and disliked exercise for its own sake. He was not some muscle-bound Adonis, and suffered from many of the ailments, including lower back pain, that afflict people as they grow older. In his remarkable life he has survived the hostility of the Antarctic and the Arctic. This is the man described as 'the world's greatest living explorer'.

Then consider sporting icons, and the difficulties they faced before reaching the top. People such as Kelly Holmes, Britain's double gold medallist in Athens, who had to endure many injury-prone years before finally achieving her dream.

The more you look at such models, the more you will overcome any perception that winners emerge only from the privileged few; that they aren't people like us. Almost certainly, they will be people like you. Be positive and tell yourself you *can* achieve your goal. Don't be negative and believe that you can't.

list your achievements

Most of us, when we look back through our lives, can find examples of small successes. There's no reason why these shouldn't be translated into something major. Reach back into your mind, remember your achievements and write them down. (This is no time for modesty; it's an occasion for total candour.) Think of your schooldays: exams passed, performances on the sports field. Then think of qualifications you have gained: before you started working and while you have been employed. What about the occasion you made a presentation at work, even if just in front of a few colleagues? And what about domestic successes – renovating your house if you happen to be a DIY fanatic, or selling and buying a flat and making a good profit? Overcoming problems, whether personal or family ones, can be considered achievements. The more you think about it, the more you will recall personal victories in the past.

Writing them down will encourage you to believe in yourself. If things get tough as you progress, you will be able to refer to them and remind yourself of what you have the potential to do.

Most achievements require self-knowledge. Once you recognize this fact, you are halfway to realizing your dreams. Ultimately, it's all about striking the vital balance between pushing yourself – entering an environment that is perhaps alien to you – and knowing what you are capable of achieving.

Redgrave's reminders

- ✔ Analyse your strengths and weaknesses – honestly.
- ✔ Decide what motivates you before you embark on your journey.
- ✔ Ask yourself how ambitious you are.
- ✔ Decide whether you are a risk-taker or a percentage player.
- ✔ Be truthful about your abilities. Otherwise you will cheat one person: yourself.

CHAPTER 3

plan to succeed

REDGRAVE'S RULE:

❝ PUSH YOURSELF TO YOUR PERSONAL LIMITS. ❞

Now that you have distilled your dreams and analysed your potential to realize them, it is time to define specific aims and set your goals.

The items on your wish list may include general goals, such as lose weight, become healthier, get fitter or make a career change. Maybe you want to run a marathon or half-marathon. Whatever your dreams, it's time to be more precise and make some serious plans. Don't worry if you still have concerns about which items are priorities on your list. There is no reason why you should not re-evaluate yourself and where you are heading at a later stage. Plenty of people change direction in midstream.

Precise targets are important because they allow you to tick boxes, to say to yourself: 'Yes, I've achieved exactly what I've set out to do.' Vagueness is the enemy of progress. It allows you to imagine that you are reaping the benefits of your strategy with no evidence that you are really doing so. If one of your dreams or goals is to lose weight, identify precisely how much and by when. Write something down, such as: 'I will lose 10 lb by 30 April.' Place the note somewhere prominent so it is always in view. The same applies if you want to change your career, set up a business or organize a fitness campaign: spell out your goal precisely.

plan to succeed

> **EXERCISE:** ROAD MAP FOR THE FUTURE
>
> Divide a sheet of paper into three columns. In the first column write down your wish list. In the second column write down the talents you already have, and link them to the dreams in your wish list. In the third column list the talents you could acquire, and again link them to specific items in your wish list. This is your road map for the future – your guide to what you want to do and what you will be able to do.

stretch yourself

I suggest you keep your goals comfortably within accessible range initially. A series of mini-goals is preferable to a major target that may quickly appear to be insurmountable. The idea is to stretch yourself, not pull yourself apart. The following example is one of many in sport that illustrates this point.

I won my first Olympic gold in 1984 at the Los Angeles Games. It was a fantastic feeling, and the pleasure was all the greater because it had been a venture into the unknown as a member of a coxed four crew that was a motley collection of characters. I remember being at the start line and thinking: 'Is this really going to be our day? Can we really be Olympic champions?' When our boat crossed the winning line first, it was a great thrill, but the main emotion I experienced was a sense of relief. We had felt we were favourites; within rowing we had been seen as favourites. Our target – Olympic gold – was within sight, and we had done what was expected of us.

In other walks of life too, all you can usually do is equal your expectations. It's only rarely that you exceed them, and when you do – if you think you're going to be third and come second – that's more exciting than winning something you're the favourite to win. The lesson here is that whatever your ambitions, it is important to keep your goals manageable and in sight. If you do better than expected, that's icing on the cake.

one step at a time

My thoughts about winning had changed radically by the time I was preparing to row at Sydney. Once I had won my fourth gold, at the Atlanta Games in 1996, I was inundated with questions, admittedly mainly from journalists, about whether I would secure an unprecedented fifth Olympic gold at consecutive Games. I had to keep reminding them that I was actually striving for one gold medal – the one that would be awarded at the next Games, in Sydney, on 23 September 2000. That was my goal. It was important that I defined what my challenge was at that particular time.

For this reason, the four previous golds and any attempts after Sydney were irrelevant. My dream was to win at the 2000 Olympic Games. Whether you are an athlete who is striving for the very

plan to succeed

top, or someone who wants to lose weight or get fitter, the principle is the same. Achieving your goal requires a focus of thought and sound planning.

In my case, winning one gold medal was an achievable goal. Thinking about it as a fifth gold, with all that this implied, would have added inevitably to the pressure I was already experiencing. I lightened my burden of expectation by viewing the Sydney gold in isolation. I refused to look back at past victories, or dwell on defeats. This is probably true of many top sportsmen and women.

I banked my past achievements in a vault in my mind, to enjoy them once I'd retired. What happened in the immediate future, and how that related to the next Olympics, was my only concern. There is no reason why everyone shouldn't do that, whatever their sphere of interest.

If I had actually set out, in my early twenties, with the aim of winning five Olympic golds, it would have seemed to be an impossible dream, too daunting a task. That's why I always regarded my challenge as the next Games and the one medal I hadn't got. One step at a time.

This all ties in with the advice in Chapter 1 to keep your dreams manageable. It is fine to have defined long-term goals, but progress is achieved far more effectively if you also have a series of mini-goals or 'stepping-stones'. (These are examined more closely in Chapter 4.) Keeping your targets in sight means that any disappointments or reverses tend to be minimized and more easily overcome.

Achieving something once is the toughest challenge. But when you succeed for the first time, you prove to yourself that there's no reason why you can't do so again. That's why I always tell young athletes that it's better to win once – as our men's rowing eight did when they won gold at Sydney – than never.

If you're planning to participate in a local half-marathon, for example, the satisfaction will be in aiming for and attaining a particular time you have set yourself. If you ran last year and came 56th, your goal will be to finish in the top 50.

There was a period in the 1980s when, through a friend of mine, I became involved in competitive bobsleighing. I even managed to win a gold medal as 'brakeman' – that's the man who pushes the bobsleigh to get it moving, then leaps in at the last moment – in the four-man bob at the 1989 British Bobsleigh Championships at Winterberg in Germany.

Two of the men who were involved with bobsleighing at the time, Gomer Lloyd and Peter Brugnani, had finished tenth in the 1984 Winter Olympics. This was just after I'd won my first Olympic gold rowing medal, and Peter told me: 'To win that gold, like you have, well, I just couldn't imagine it. When we crossed the line and the scoreboard flashed up and we discovered that we were tenth, we couldn't believe it. We were jumping for joy all over the place.' The reason Gomer and Peter were so ecstatic was that they had done far better than they had expected, given the elite competition.

The point is that everything you do has to be placed in context…like a retired rower running a marathon. By the time you read this, I hope to have taken part in my second London Marathon and beaten the time I recorded in the first. Marathon running isn't just for the elite. Yes, it is a tough exercise – but I believe it's achievable by nearly everybody.

countdown to the london marathon

This is my guide to planning a London Marathon run.

1. Self-assessment

Assess the physical shape you're in and the condition you're starting from. At the beginning of the year, having been out of competitive sport for four years, my level of fitness was – from my own perspective – very poor, although most people planning to do the marathon for fun would have regarded it as very high. From the very beginning of the year I could run reasonably hard for an hour, not far off the pace that I would run a marathon, and not get out of breath.

2. Routine

As you approach the marathon, you should be getting into a routine. It's all about increasing the distance covered and getting your body used to the fatigue. When you are certain that you are ready to run, with about three months left to train, start assessing: 'What do I want to get out of this marathon? Is it mere completion? Is it a set time?' Based on what you decide, set a training schedule that fits your domestic routine and takes into account your progress.

3. Aims

What time should you aim for? I'd say four to five hours is acceptable. To achieve that, you need to do five running sessions a week. To decide on distances and times, work backwards from what your aim is on the day (see 'Planning for action', page 59).

4. Practice

A month before the event do a half-marathon – about 20 km (12 miles) – at the pace you want to run in the big race. Clock the distance and time. To work out the distance, use a pedometer, or retrace the route you ran by car, which is what I do.

Two weeks before the marathon, you should run a three-quarters distance, or about 30 km (18 miles). That is the really horrible one. It's the longest run you'll do, apart from the marathon itself.

5. Repeat

A week before the event, you should be running a quarter distance of a full marathon – about 10 km (6 miles) – at slightly above the pace you want to race. By then you should have worked out the pace with which you're comfortable.

The final week won't involve a lot of work. It's more about recovery and ensuring that you possess the right energy levels for the day itself.

6. Pace yourself

On the day itself, remember that marathon running is all about pacing. Go off too hard, and you'll really struggle. Ideally, aim for a slower pace in the first half, then pick up speed. I'd like to see the route marked out in kilometres. The markers come along quicker, so there's more chance to assess the pace you're running at. Because there's such a fun atmosphere, you tend to go off a lot quicker than you should. That decision can come back to haunt you.

The first time I did the London Marathon was in 2001, when I was also the official starter; then completion was good enough for me, the time was unimportant. I'd never done anything more than a half-marathon before. My wife Ann and I had decided to run the marathon together, and she was slowed down by a blister on her foot that turned into an abscess. I knew I was going to do it again when I could concentrate more on the time. I am aiming for around four hours in 2005.

set precise goals

Success in sport, in business – and in life generally – rarely happens spontaneously. Behind every triumph, whether by a team or an individual, there is generally significant planning and a structure. Whether in sport or other aspects of life, it is absolutely crucial to set precise goals that may be tough, but are achievable. Chapter 7 looks at the manner in which Sir Clive Woodward transformed England's Rugby Union team into World Cup winners in 2003. It is a classic example of how one man had a dream, set his goals and planned the process meticulously.

Once you have established your goal, you need an action plan. Write precisely what the goal is – as discussed earlier – then formulate a strategy to reach it. And remember: small steps can lead to a giant success.

Someone seeking to lose weight needs to calculate the amount of weight they need to shed each week to achieve their target. If they reduce this to a small loss per day, it may be manageable without radical reductions in diet. They then need to work out how they are going to achieve that loss – what would be left out of their diet, allied to a fitness schedule. Planning their strategy that way should remove one great worry: fear of failure.

PLANNING FOR ACTION

Objective: Whatever your goal, it is always an excellent idea to work back from it. Write down precisely what your aim is.

Steps to take: What are the stages you will progress through to arrive at your goal?

Timetable: Writing your own timetable is perhaps the best way to discipline yourself. You may feel this is not necessary, but I suggest you do it anyway.

Following these steps is obviously particularly beneficial when you are plotting a sporting goal. If you are attempting a marathon or half-marathon, you would write: 'On [date] I will run [42 km/26 miles or 20 km/12 miles] under a time of [whatever you decide].'

Then work backwards, giving yourself not only targets in terms of distances and times for each month up until then, but also a calendar of dates when you will train, and even details of your diet.

In the same way, you could create an action plan for losing weight, buying a house, or completing a degree course. What is important is to have an action plan, and stick to it.

break everything down into achievable chunks

My favourite example of how small steps can have the same effect as one giant stride is the story of how the American swimmer John Naber improved remarkably as an international swimmer by planning his goals effectively.

John, whose event was the 100-metre backstroke, made the 1972 Olympics. He was part of the US relay team that qualified for the final, but after helping the team to this stage by participating in the heats and semi-final, he found his place usurped. The big boys – Mike Stamm, Tom Bruce, Mark Spitz and Jerry Heidenreich – came in, raced the final and won. Understandably, he was disappointed that he wasn't standing on the rostrum with a medal.

As he prepared for the 1976 Games at Montreal, John was determined that he would not just be part of the relay team, but would try to win his individual event. However, he recognized that this would mean groundbreaking performances and reaching new targets that had never been reached before. How could he achieve that?

He looked through the record books and discovered that there had been a steady improvement in times in successive Olympics. Performances might dip slightly immediately after each Games, but they would then steadily improve and attain a new high a year before the next Olympics. At the Games themselves, the gold medallists invariably won in a new world's best time. John felt he could predict the time in which the gold medal would be won in 1976, a time that would enable him to beat the German competitor who had won the two previous Olympics. That time was 55.5 seconds. John's problem was that his personal best was 59.5 seconds. He had to find four seconds from somewhere – over 100 metres, swimming on his back. In the swimming pool that's a huge time difference. He felt there was no way he was going to do it. He actually moved away from the sport for a short period.

Then he started to look at swimming in a different way. He said to himself: 'OK, I've got four seconds to find, but I haven't got to do it this week, or this month. I've got nearly four years to do it.' He broke the time down to a second a year, and as he trained for ten months a year, that was a tenth of a second a month. Assuming there were 30 days in a month, that would be 300th of a second each day. He trained for four hours a day, every day. He'd therefore have to make 1200th of a second improvement every hour.

Apparently it takes 5/1200th of a second for an eye to blink, so he was looking for an improvement of 1/5th of the blink of an eye in every hour's training. He thought: 'That's got to be the way to do it: break it down so that each increment of improvement is attainable.' It was by no means simple to make that improvement every training hour of every day of every month for four years. But that's what he did. He made the US Olympic team, qualified for the individual event, and won the gold in 55.49 seconds – almost identical to the target he'd set himself. For good measure, he also won other events, including the 100-metre medley.

When setting his goals, John was also establishing his strategy. He formulated a plan of campaign. He established that you need a long-term goal, but that setting short-term targets is part of the process of achieving it. It is essential to break everything down so that you can do things in achievable chunks.

In other words, the key is to transform a goal that appears daunting, impossible even, into something you can do without really thinking about it. It becomes a matter of routine – provided there's a structure behind that routine. As he divided the four-second time difference into tiny parts, it didn't take a lot of excess energy to achieve what he set out to do.

John is now one of the USA's premier motivational speakers.

MAKE YOUR MIND WORK FOR YOU

Possessing ability is one thing; being able to harness that talent at a particular time is quite another. There are numerous individuals and teams who struggle to produce their best performances at major championships. Just consider Arsenal, who in the last couple of years have dominated the Premiership, but in Europe have constantly failed at that highest level, sometimes being defeated by lesser teams.

They provide a good example of how the mind can work negatively. As Arsenal's manager Arsène Wenger has admitted, the team's imperious displays in domestic competition have raised everyone's expectations – not just their supporters', but the team's too. As he says: 'I feel we want to deliver so much. When you always feel you have to do that, you are less relaxed and not so good. The problem is that we have not yet developed the same confidence level in the Champions League as the Premiership.'

think laterally

The principles behind John Naber's achievement can be adapted to suit any goal in any walk of life. The lesson is that you don't always have to approach your goals from the most obvious perspective. Of course, making improvements need not just be about time. In a team sport it's about fitness and skill-based training, and blending those elements together in a structure that allows progress to be measured on a week-to-week, month-to-month basis.

In business the same principles can be utilized to analyse and improve your monthly sales figures. 'I *just* achieved my target last month; how am I going to repeat that?' is a constant source of concern in offices everywhere. The key is to break everything down and make sure the day is structured effectively. Break it into sections to ensure that the use of time is more efficient. Ask yourself questions. For example, are your team doing enough preparatory work so that phone calls aren't wasted? Are they targeting customers effectively?

Let's imagine you want a 10 per cent increase on sales: work backwards from your goal, and break it all up into small chunks. If, for example, you set out to achieve £125,000 in a year, the target feels more manageable if you calculate that it is the equivalent of making about £2,403 a week, or just over £480 a day. Psychologically, this seems less overwhelming and much more attainable than your long-term goal.

Whatever challenge you face, view it from different perspectives before embarking on it. Say you have decided on a new career or life change. Use visualization to imagine yourself in that situation. What does it feel like? It may help if you write down your feelings.

Now allow your mind to work backwards, and, as you do so, divide that goal into achievable stages. If you have a career change in mind, you might need to spend a certain amount of time taking courses and gaining experience.

A LATERAL APPROACH TO CAREER CHANGE

Why not set yourself targets in the same way that pilots log their flying hours? That's the technique used by one of our brightest young football managers, Alex Inglethorpe, whose non-league team Exeter City famously held Manchester United to a draw at Old Trafford in the 2004/5 FA Cup.

When, at 28, Alex decided to quit playing and go into coaching and management, he had already embarked on various courses to gain the necessary qualifications. Just as importantly however, he set himself the task of logging as many coaching sessions as he could out on the training pitch with players. He continues to view as many games as possible, and talks to experienced managers whenever he can. He didn't merely think: 'I fancy being a football manager. Let's see what happens.' His career is planned out.

While he'll need to demonstrate man-managing talent to succeed at the top level, and have a certain amount of luck, his preparation is an ideal model of what we should all do if planning a career change.

In athletics, competitors are looking to achieve fractions of seconds improvements over 100 metres to improve the world record. Increasingly, all sportsmen and women are conditioned to win by these margins. Just recall the victory of Great Britain's men's 4 × 100 metre sprint relay team by 1/100th of a second at the Athens' Olympics. And what of Kelly Holmes's triumph in the 1500 metres by 5/100th of a second? In the velodrome, cyclist Chris Hoy won his 1 km time trial by 138/1000th of a second. There was not much more than the length of a handlebar between first and second place at the end of his event.

By contrast, when someone breaks the marathon world record they tend to do so by relatively long margins. But as time goes on, it's likely that people will be looking for improvements of fractions of a second even in that discipline.

set your own gold times and standards

In my motivational talks to sports-related and business audiences, I adapt the John Naber story to explain how the Great Britain rowing squad goes about training. Our sport is endurance-based, so it's a slightly different concept; but there are similarities in that we look to reduce the time of our performances between Olympics.

As I mentioned in Chapter 1, the Great Britain rowing coach Jurgen Grobler always set 'gold' times – in other words, targets he believed should be achieved if the boat were to have a chance of winning an Olympic gold medal. His aim in training was that we

plan to succeed

should shave seconds off our times without putting in any extra effort. The theory is that if you can do this at low and intermediate levels, by the time you reach your pinnacle, in the Olympic final, the capacity is there to bring out the performance you want. If you get your basics correct at a low level, the discipline will carry you through to top.

ENDURANCE TRAINING

Meet up: 7.30 a.m. in summer, 8 a.m. in winter.

First training session: Out on the water, rowing 20–24 km (12–14 miles), which took just under two hours, depending on the category of boat. The work would be very much low endurance, with a 'holding' heart rate at somewhere between 120 and 140 beats per minute.

That could change, depending on the stage of the season. Normally, when we started training again after our three-week break following a world championship or Olympics, we'd do single sculls. Then, after Christmas, we'd move into pairs and fours. In springtime we'd move into an eight, just to avoid monotony.

Second session: Having taken a break for some 'fuel' – fluids and food – we'd probably go back out on the water and complete another 16–20 km (10–12 miles). This second session would be a bit more intensive, with a heart rate of 130–150, sometimes 160, beats per minute.

Alternatively, the second session could be in the gym, doing a muscular weights circuit with 13–15 different stations and a number of different exercises and repetitions before moving on.

Our gym sessions were among our most intensive training sessions, and produced quite a lot of lactic acid, a substance that effectively safeguards the body from overuse. Essentially, it acts as a valve, slowing the body down so that it does not overwork and thus damage itself. This kind of training regime is scientifically-based, trying to push the thresholds of the lactate higher so that we could put more load on our bodies without the lactic acid kicking in and trying to slow it down. Most training for rowing is endurance-based, which is just below the threshold where lactic acid is produced.

This, of course, was science applied to international sport. What I want to emphasize is that it is vital to set yourself precise goals and create a structure in which you can work efficiently. Many of your goals clearly won't involve the production of lactic acid, but it does no harm to view your progress in similar terms. It's a useful analogy because to achieve your goals you will need to push yourself to new levels – but at a sensible rate. Overdoing it would simply be destructive.

Our training was designed to avoid monotony, and this is also a vital part of planning for your goals. While routine is important (see Chapter 6), sheer repetitive tasks can be mind-numbingly dull and demotivating. Variety is as crucial to your planning as it is in a box of chocolates. Everyone needs new and different challenges to maintain their desire and enthusiasm – as many people in the workplace will readily testify.

the sydney challenge

We started planning for the 2000 Sydney Olympics immediately after the Atlanta Games – four years in advance – working back on a year-by-year basis. We had everything mapped out: where we wanted to go and how we planned to get there. We were meticulous, but our plan always allowed for alternatives if injury interrupted our strategy – as indeed it did. It was never a matter of training each day and thinking: 'What are we going to do today?' At our level we could never have survived with ad hoc preparation. This was our strategy:

1 At 10.30 a.m. on Penrith Lake, just outside Sydney, on 23 September 2000, the coxless fours final was going to take place.
2 One boat was going to win.
3 We predicted that under the best possible conditions the victorious boat would have to record a time of 5 minutes 41 seconds to cross the line first.
4 We also anticipated that the conditions wouldn't be perfect. The prevailing winds were headwinds, so times would be slower than predicted. However, physically we had to be in the right shape to achieve that time. And physically and mentally we had to be conditioned to do it.

It's like setting a course on board a ship or aircraft. We knew where we wanted to be at a certain time, and instead of a setting a strategy that worked forward to that time, we worked back from it.

We asked ourselves the following questions:

- On the day of the final, what would be the best training session to do as a warm-up?
- What would we do the day before?
- How did we want to race the semi-final two days before that?
- How long did we want to spend in the Olympic village preparing for the first race in order to get used to the atmosphere and a new environment, acclimatize to weather conditions and recover from the travelling?

Then we traced our journey back home:

- What training camps would we complete before going to Australia?
- What altitude training would we complete?
- Which regattas would we take part in, in the build-up?

Then we went back to winter training:

- What small trials would we do?
- What assessments would we want to do?

As outlined here, our strategy might sound obvious, but many people fail to structure the route to their goal effectively, and they tend to forget that improvement does not normally occur in mighty bounds. It happens in small steps, and these may not be in a straight line. This is discussed in Chapter 4, but for the moment concentrate on your precise goals and how you plan to achieve them.

plan to succeed

Redgrave's reminders

✔ Set yourself precise goals.
✔ Stretch yourself, but keep your goals manageable and in sight.
✔ Break everything down into achievable chunks.
✔ Focus on what is possible.
✔ Once you have succeeded for the first time, you have proved to yourself that there's no reason why you can't do so again.
✔ Set your own gold standards.

CHAPTER 4

be flexible and use stepping-stones

REDGRAVE'S RULE:

❝ **PROGRESS DOESN'T ALWAYS HAPPEN IN A STRAIGHT LINE.** ❞

You've defined your goals and decided on your strategy to go about realizing your dreams. That's fine in an ideal world. But remember, there's more than one way to achieve what you have set out to do.

Leaping across a stream with a single bound is the quickest way to reach the other side, but using individual stepping-stones will give you the flexibility, physical and mental, to pause and reflect – and possibly make a better choice. It may be a disjointed way of crossing, but sometimes it's the safest and, ultimately, the most satisfying. You do not necessarily have to travel towards a goal in a straight line. Sometimes you may have to deviate – in the real world things never go smoothly – and adjust to new situations at particular times. If problems crop up and you're faced with the unexpected or feel pressurized, look on the challenges as stepping-stones that will allow you to re-evaluate and adapt your abilities.

I had to adapt my career when I learnt that I had contracted colitis, and again when I was a diagnosed as a diabetic. It was in the build-up to the 1992 Barcelona Olympics that I was told I had colitis, a debilitating disease of the colon. My performances had deteriorated to such a degree that Matthew Pinsent, my then

be flexible

partner in the coxless pair, and coach Jurgen Grobler sat down and talked about it.

With the games fast approaching, Jurgen told Matthew that if things didn't change in the next couple of weeks, something radical would have to be done. The brutal truth was that Matthew would have to find somebody else to row with or move into another boat. He, remember, was absolutely fit. He had to get the best out of the situation in both the short and long term. If either option had been decided on, Matthew would have needed to be flexible enough to deal with it. I would have found it hard to take, but I would have understood. Fortunately, such drastic action wasn't required. I received treatment, recovered and was fit enough to take part. We won the gold medal with something to spare.

From a team perspective, the build-up of our coxless four for Sydney in 2000 was even worse. There can be no better example of the need for separate and individual 'stepping-stones', even though there were times when I thought we might slip into the rushing stream. Tim Foster severed a tendon on the back of his hand and an operation was required to repair it; I contracted diabetes; James had a difficult break up with his girlfriend. We could not have predicted that these things would happen when we developed our original plan of campaign so meticulously.

Yet we overcame those problems by dealing with them separately – each as an individual stepping stone – and adapting to them.

nothing is written in stone

Tim's injury was our first dilemma. How much time should we allow him to get over his operation and return to the Sydney-bound four? While Time recovered, Luka Grubor came in as a substitute. On paper the change appeared to work quite well. In training we actually seemed to be faster with Luka in the boat than Tim. But when it came to races, it wasn't the same. Jurgen decided that we shouldn't persevere with Luka and that we'd wait for Tim to recover. But how long should we wait?

As it turned out, it was only a short time before Tim was ready again, but had the operation not been successful, we would have had to reassess our options once again as we viewed the bigger picture of trying to win the Sydney Olympics.

We had a similar problem when Ed Coode was in the boat after Tim was sidelined with a serious back problem that required surgery. We were performing as well, if not better, than when Tim was in the boat. The best world championship I ever experienced was at St Katherine's in Canada with Ed in the crew. It was another problem for Jurgen. Had he believed that Ed should remain in the boat, he would have been tough enough to make that decision. However, as has been well chronicled, Tim eventually made it to Sydney.

The stepping-stone approach gave us the flexibility to navigate around these problems and still claim that Olympic gold medal. The same applies to anyone with specific goals. To achieve your ambitions you must have a strategy to re-evaluate and reassess the situation as you progress.

be flexible

The route you actually take may be very different from the path and strategy you decided on when you set out to reach your goal. You must have the flexibility, of mind and body, to adapt to circumstances as you travel to your final destination. This is a very important factor in realizing your dreams. Remember, nothing is written in stone.

keep your eye on the big prize

In the rowing world you race in a certain number of regattas a year. In an ideal world you want to win them. Other success criteria may not be to win necessarily, but to give the best possible performance and attempt to improve on it next time. In Chapter 3 I mentioned the Sydney gold of the Great Britain eight. They didn't win anything in the build-up to the 2000 Games, yet they walked away with an Olympic gold. In their case, it could be said that they didn't so much use stepping-stones as walk on crazy paving! But it worked for them.

I imagine that in the original build-up the Great Britain eight would have liked to win all their World Cup races and Henley Royal Regatta events, but they didn't. They were consistently on the podium, but rarely on top. In fact, they were beaten by five separate countries on a regular basis during the build-up to the Games. What was crucial, however, was that they all believed they were good enough to win the Olympics. They had their own strategy, and it proved to be successful, even though it was very different from ours.

be flexible

WHAT HAPPENS WHEN YOU DON'T ADAPT

Many believe that the England football coach Sven-Goran Eriksson was guilty of a failure to adapt during the last World Cup. Before the Japan–South Korea game David Beckham damaged his foot. You no doubt recall the debate about his fractured metatarsal bone and whether the England captain was sufficiently fit to play.

It meant a drastic re-evaluation of the situation. Eriksson must have had some doubts as to whether Beckham should have travelled in the first place. Having decided that he should, I am sure that Eriksson would have been assessing the situation as the team arrived in the Far East, remaining flexible in his approach. As England coach, his first priority was to select the best players, but it was equally crucial that all of them should be fit, healthy and on top form.

In Japan, the reality was that although Beckham was playing again, he wasn't at his best by any means. Eriksson evidently believed that the captain's mere presence as a 'talisman' compensated for any lack of fitness. With hindsight, it is easy to say that his decision was wrong, but had Beckham performed at his best, or with even a glimmer of brilliance, and England had gone further in the World Cup, Eriksson would have been hailed as a genius.

This episode should serve as a warning that the best-laid plans may need revising. You must always be prepared to change course midstream.

be flexible

always reassess

It is important to reassess your situation constantly. You must be prepared to be flexible, both physically and mentally, to adjust to conditions as they come up. Chapter 1 discussed being realistic. Here we meet that word again: you must be realistic about your progress – and that requires total honesty.

In rowing there are different physical tests, and in particular the ergo (the rowing machine), so it's very easy to assess the kind of form you are in. It's a very visual part of training. It is important to establish your progress by whatever means you prefer. Gut instinct won't get you very far with this, and if things have become tough, it's easy but unhelpful to get down on yourself. The answer is to assess rationally why you haven't maintained the standard you require. You may have been at a low ebb, perhaps through illness, and haven't given as good a performance as your original plan had anticipated. You may have put in a lot of work, but still haven't achieved a particular goal.

Let's return to our weight-loss example. You've hit the wall, so to speak. In your quest to shed 12 kg (2 stone) in a year, you started well – a few pounds disappeared – but now, three months in, those accursed scales are sticking obstinately around the same weight. It's dispiriting, and you're tempted to quit now. That's the easy decision, but the wrong one.

With weight loss, as with a fitness regime, it's a common fault to attempt too much too soon, only to discover that the upward curve of progress soon levels off. That's why I always advocate a gradual, steady approach from the start. However, it does no harm to reassess your progress at regular intervals.

If you have come to a frustrating halt on the scales, it may be time to take stock. Give yourself a diet break for a day or two (that doesn't mean binge-eating), and having a hard look at your strategy. Can you see ways of improving your regime? Should you be combining the diet with a fitness programme involving some regular exercise – even if it's only walking? Does your diet need some alteration? Does your plan need restructuring so that it becomes more achievable? Maybe your target date should be put back, especially if you are being too ambitious. Perhaps, as an extra incentive, you should introduce a reward for each stage reached. Some people respond well to that.

Conversely, your programme could be too easy for you. In the long term that achieves very little. Think of yourself as a high-jumper who constantly leaps the same height. That would indicate excellence, but only at a certain level. Could you improve on that? Again, it's time for honesty. Are you really pushing yourself to reach the next stage? Or are you in a comfort zone? If the latter, the chances are that you've set your bar too low.

Make sure you assess yourself over a period of weeks or months, not days. If you're a sportsman or woman, there's no point in doing just one easy training session, then immediately saying: 'That was too simple. I've got to reassess my programme. Tomorrow I've got to do twice as much.' Build up gradually and be realistic about the length of time it takes to see an improvement.

be flexible

The same applies to a weight-loss or fitness regime. You have to analyse your progress over weeks or months, not days. Similarly, if you are running your own business, you wouldn't start panicking or, conversely, reinvesting all your anticipated profits on the basis of one month's trading. You'd assess your progress over six months minimum.

It's all a question of balance. James Cracknell, a member of our victorious Sydney four and a gold medallist in the four at Athens, frequently thought training had been 'too easy' on a particular day. He always wanted to do more to complete a training session. Sometimes he'd go to the local gym and do extra training by himself. In his own mind this was to make up for what we, as a crew, hadn't done. By the end of the following week he'd be absolutely shattered and wouldn't be able to complete a training session. In some ways, this is not a bad attitude to have, but in my view it's not a particularly productive one either!

This is why you have to assess your schedule in terms of what you're actually trying to achieve. And that's why 'Planning for action' on page 59 is an essential tool in your progress towards achieving your goal. It will keep you focused on what you have or haven't achieved at any given time. In most activities you have hard weeks and easy weeks. In rowing, it was all about coming to a peak at the time of a regatta.

It has also become clear to me that a similar truth applies to the business world, and often to life in general. In this section I will talk about making your mind work for you through a variety of means – the different stepping-stones that will help you to achieve your goal.

be prepared to be flexible

The subject of flexibility has already been discussed under the headings of setting goals and planning and structuring your route – all long-term strategies. Yet it is just as vital to be prepared for the unexpected in the shorter term – when you actually arrive in a competitive situation or when you need to make an impression in the workplace.

Let me give you an example of this. After it was decided that Barcelona would host the 1992 Olympic Games, Matthew and I went to Spain every February and trained at Banyoles, the location of the rowing regatta. It was a good training base, but it was also the Olympic venue, so we were able to get used to it. It became a home from home. We became familiar with the lake and its idiosyncrasies, and thus reduced the likelihood of any nasty surprises.

Surprises are not what you want when you're favourites for an event. Yes, I know, they are loved by the public, and therefore by the media because a surprise makes a good story; but a suprise means almost invariably that something untoward has happened to the favourite.

I find it strange that in Britain we're such great lovers of the underdog. Unless we are supporters of a particular team, we like seeing the more talented team, the one with more ability, being beaten. I was like that myself as a child. Not any more. Maybe the reason I can't quite understand the logic of this attitude is because the crews I rowed in were frequently favourites for an event. Usually, favourites are defeated only when they under-perform – often because

be flexible

they are caught out by a surprise. I worked hard to ensure that didn't happen.

How did I do that? Within the overall strategy, you have to have a frame of mind that *expects the unexpected*. You have to *anticipate and adapt* to situations, and not *react* to them.

This is a particularly important in business. Imagine a few years ago you had been involved in running one of the first mobile phone companies: your primary concern would have been whether the product could be used efficiently for one-to-one calls. Today mobiles are all-singing, all-dancing pieces of equipment that can be used as still cameras, video cameras, radios, music players and televisions.

Those original manufacturers of mobiles would have been quickly overtaken and possibly put out of business if they hadn't invested millions in research and development *and*, just as crucially, maintained a very close eye on their rivals. They would never have become the billion-pound corporations they are today if they'd sat back and said: 'Nobody will ever produce moving pictures on a mobile telephone.'

Their strategy was rather like Matthew's and mine before a race: they had answers before the problems occurred.

This strategy applies to all businesses, whatever the size. In commercial terms, complacency can be a killer. Just think of the recent struggles endured by Sainsbury's, formerly the UK's favourite supermarket, and the huge profits currently enjoyed by Tesco, which has overtaken it.

Expecting the unexpected is also an important concept for an employee within the workplace, particularly in job or promotion

be flexible

interviews. We all tend to prepare for the questions we'd like to be asked, when it would actually be better to anticipate those we'd rather not. For example, what are your weaker areas that might make you unsuitable for the job? Can you turn those weaknesses into strengths, or perhaps deflect attention from them so that they go unnoticed? This means remaining positive rather than defensive. By all means rehearse in your mind what you probably *will* be asked, but follow up with questions that probably *won't* feature in the interview, but could prove decidedly tricky if they do. The motto 'Be prepared' is as relevant in the workplace as the scout camp.

Some teams and coaches are fine when all is going well and working smoothly; but when things start to get a bit disjointed they rapidly fall apart. They don't have the know-how or flexibility within their thought processes to get over the problems. Everything becomes destructive rather than constructive.

The fact is, in general terms, lesser performers always attempt to raise their standards against the favourites. It's the familiar FA Cup giant-killer strategy. The Davids may have less talent, but they profit from the advantages they do have: a home fixture with vociferous support, a dodgy surface, usually an element of good fortune, and the all-important aspect: complacent Goliaths. Every year managers of the elite clubs chant their mantras: 'We won't underestimate the opposition'; 'We'll give them the respect they deserve'; 'It's 11 versus 11'; 'We know that nine times out of ten we'll beat them. We've got to ensure that this isn't the tenth.' The warnings are all there, yet virtually every year someone fails to follow them through and the underdogs come out on top.

be flexible

worrying can be good for you

Think of worrying as one form of looking ahead, a kind of preparation that will lessen the chances of something unexpected happening. Think of nerves as a positive force that can actually give you an edge in a pressurized situation.

WINNERS WORRY TOO

When I was first on the international sports scene I used to watch those outstanding British athletes Steve Ovett and Seb Coe on the start line. Like many people, I harboured an inherent belief that they were unbeatable. Yet Seb somehow always looked nervous. He was always twitching. I used to think to myself: 'What's Seb worried about? Why is he doing that? I know he's going to win, and so does everybody else watching the race on TV: thousands of people around the world.' He obviously felt he should win, but he was still very nervous about whether he would.

I failed to understand this until I was in the same situation – until I was in the position of being favourite. As favourite, you can't do better than match up to everybody's expectation. You may perform to your optimum capabilities, but in terms of results, the best you can do is win and equal those expectations. Your mind therefore finds other things to worry about.

Events at Henley were ones we were expected to win – comfortably. Certainly, when Matthew and I were doing the pair together, competing for the Silver Goblets, the first rounds were always pretty straightforward, at least on paper. We'd be up against university crews, who might have had potential but weren't in our class.

But when we were on the start line on the first day I'd be distracted by possible faults in the boat's equipment. I'd think: 'I hope this rigger's going to hold on; I hope this gate's not going to break. I wonder how strong these oars are.' I worried, for the sake of worrying. It was ridiculous because once we were up against strong opposition, I didn't think about the boat or the equipment. When you're rowing in a race you don't think about any external influences; they're just taken for granted.

The point is, you have to worry about something. But that's no bad thing. Worry is an important emotion on the start line. If you take things too much for granted, you can get caught out by something unexpected happening. If you achieve one good performance, there is a tendency to believe you will be able to do so again and again. But too often complacency can intrude.

This can be seen in many sporting scenarios.

emphasize the positive

You may well pose the question: 'Just a minute, Steve. If I worry too much on the start line, or lining up a golf shot, or preparing for a project at work, won't it simply place me under more pressure? Won't that be

be flexible

detrimental?' It is true that if you allow it to dominate, pressure can damage your performance. This is negative pressure. Used effectively, pressure can enhance your output. That is positive pressure. I've learnt over the years that to become a winner you must thrive on pressure – make it positive and exploit it to your advantage; not let it destroy you.

THE PRESSURE'S ON

Grace under pressure is a highly desirable quality, so be alert to the situations that can affect you for good or bad.

Positive pressures:
- Stimulate you and give you an edge.
- Keep the mind sharp.
- Make you hungry and keep you determined.
- Keep you keenly aware of the opposition, but not in awe or fear of them.

Negative pressures:
- Make you want to escape and hide from the challenge ahead.
- Are so overwhelming that they can diminish you physically and impair your thinking.
- Make you act irrationally.

Professional football offers many examples of behaviour under pressure. Look at Wayne Rooney, Manchester United's striker, playing against his former team, Everton. Like any footballer, when he is fired up and determined because of a particular challenge, he is a potential asset to his team. That is a positive reaction to pressure. Sometimes, however, negative pressure takes hold of the teenager, and he becomes hot-headed and ill-disciplined, and backchats to referees. He receives unnecessary cautions, which create a distraction and lessen his impact on a game.

People who perform badly often blame the pressure of the situation they're in. They shouldn't. Unless someone is absolutely riddled with quivering nerves, pressure should be a benefit, not a hindrance. After every competition victorious athletes say things such as, 'I was so nervous beforehand' as though this was something to be admitted with a sense of guilt, as though the person concerned was not a true professional. There is a false expectation that all sportsmen should become 'The Iceman' in a high-pressure situation.

The fact is, you *should* be nervous when you are pressurized, whether in sport, giving a business presentation that could win you a promotion, or simply driving along a motorway in bad weather. This is an important part of human nature; part of survival. It is the adrenalin response. It goes back to the era of the caveman when it was kill or die. Human beings had to be flexible, able to react instantly to changes in their environment. Nerves meant that all their senses were sharper so that they were acutely aware of the close proximity of predators and could take action against them. If man had been created to be blasé about such perils, he would never have survived.

be flexible

Even towards the end of my career I suffered from nerves. If anything, they got worse. But they are part of the body chemistry that makes people winners. The adrenalin keeps them on their toes and ensures that they avoid becoming complacent.

use pressure as a stepping-stone

Basic skills are, of course, vital to success. If you don't have the ability to perform whatever task you're given you won't ever succeed. But how you cope when you're under pressure is equally important.

THE PRESSURE ELEMENT

Noel Hunt, a very good golf professional, gave exhibition performances for a living. He could strike a ball as well as anyone, but he didn't make the top grade on the circuit. At a Ryder Cup opening a few years ago, he walked along a line of balls, hitting them unerringly by swinging two clubs, backwards and forwards. Also as part of the show, he'd get a putter out and, striking a ball with the smooth face, put a draw or a fade on it, and drive it accurately 225 metres (250 yards) plus.

Afterwards, he attempted a simple putt – and missed it. The message is: 'There is a lot more to golf than just being able to strike a ball. There's the element of pressure, too.'

be flexible

Most top golfers can drive a golf ball on demand with any club in their bag, even a putter. But Peter Alliss, who for many years has been a BBC golf commentator, was one player who had the reputation of not having the best short game. The truth is, of course, that top golfers like him can putt; they are physically capable of it. What they can't necessarily do is cope with pressure. This is true of some of the greatest golfers. Indeed, it is the essence of golf. Players practise the physical actions endlessly with their coaches, but often it is what is going on in their minds – their reaction to pressure on the day – that determines the success or otherwise of a shot.

At a lesser level, I understand the feeling myself. I get it all the time when I play in charity golf games. People say: 'This is a pressure putt, Steve; you're the man for this.' Well, yes. I could cope if I were in a rowing boat on the morning of a final at an Olympic regatta because I would have prepared for the event over months, even years. But as an enthusiastic amateur golfer, whose preparation has been minimal, trying to sink a 2-metre (6-foot) putt to give my team points in a charity tournament…. That's a different matter entirely.

You may interrupt at this point and say: 'Well, that's fine, Steve, but you're talking about a charity tournament on the golf course. It doesn't really matter whether you win or lose. My aims and ambitions are rather more important than that. They affect my whole family. What about the pressure then?'

Of course, this is true. However, what should not be forgotten is that dealing with pressure in sport, and being flexible enough to use it to your advantage, can be similar to dealing with pressure in the workplace. The lessons to be learnt are often the same.

If, say, you're a salesperson, stress levels can be high as you approach the cut-off time for producing your monthly figures. You know you have to reach your target, and it's inevitable that your anxiety will increase. Don't let the pressure get you down. Adapt to it and use it. Let it drive you to double-check your figures, rethink client contacts and make that extra, last-minute effort. Similarly, if you have to give a company presentation, you may worry about whether you have prepared everything correctly and whether you are going to make the right impression. Be positive: instead of just worrying, make absolutely sure that you're well prepared – the confidence this gives you will ensure that you make a good impression.

fight the negatives

I am well aware of the difficulties of speaking in public. Not just in front of work colleagues, but also when I'm confronted by the mass media. The public speaking I do inspired this book, and these days I am confident about it. But addressing hundreds, sometimes thousands, of people was not something that came naturally to me: as a youngster, I was really quite shy. The same is true of many people, yet at some time most of us have had to stand up and speak in front of other people, even if only as best man at a wedding.

Public speaking provides a good example of fighting the negatives; of believing you can do something when all the evidence in your own mind, and possibly the minds of others, suggests you can't. Of course, to combat nerves requires flexibility in your approach to yourself. A visualization exercise will help here. Start by playing your mental DVD player and see yourself as a success: being congratulated after giving a presentation, coming first in a race, making a speech fluently and with confidence. Then run through all the possible negative pressures that achieving your goal could involve. Replace each one with its opposite – positive pressure – and play these on your mental screen.

I remember appearing with Roger Black, the Olympic 400-metre silver medallist, who in his retirement has developed into a highly professional television presenter and motivational speaker. He is a good-looking fellow with a great personality, and was a fine sportsman. He came on stage and talked about the Team Visa scheme we'd just launched. He'd picked it up really quickly and presented it very well indeed. His polished performance made me think: 'I wish I could speak like that.'

Despite feeling a bit negative about myself, I made my presentation and it went quite well. Later, however, I talked to somebody who said: 'I enjoyed your style because you were natural.' This was a useful lesson for me: it made me realize that even though I didn't have a natural talent for public speaking, I could still succeed.

This is a good example of fighting negatives. At some time or other we're bound to hear, probably from our own critical mind: 'You aren't up to that' or 'You don't have the right kind of character for that.' Don't you believe it. Human beings are remarkably adaptable.

Say you have given a presentation at work, and as you drive home, you are thinking: 'Well, I made a complete mess of that.

be flexible

I forgot where I was halfway through that story, and that joke didn't get a laugh.' This may all be true, but there must be some aspects of the presentation that you were pleased with. Ask yourself what they were. Your inner voice might say: 'Well, everyone listened attentively. I think I did get my message across. And though I didn't get that story right, my mistake did make everyone chuckle. Overall the rapport was good.'

Whatever activity is involved, whether addressing a conference or climbing a mountain, fight the negatives by refusing to dwell on what might go wrong and concentrating instead on what could go well. If you're not completely happy with your performance, learn from the negatives and think positive. Think: 'Next time, it can only get better.'

MY OWN NEGATIVE PRESSURE

My biggest worry when I'm playing golf, especially in a major charity game, is not about playing in front of the many spectators these events attract, but that I might actually hit them from close range. Very occasionally, I take a swing and hit it off the toe of the club, making the ball go off at right angles. I don't do it often – perhaps once a season on average – but being conscious that it could happen fills me with negative pressure. In this case, I try to practise what I preach and focus on a positive outcome.

always be yourself

On another occasion I was asked to give a talk to an American company based in Britain. We all know about American presentations, and how smooth and 'professional' they are. Afterwards someone said: 'That wasn't the slickest performance I've ever heard, but there was a passion about the way you talked. You obviously believed in what you put across.' I realized this was actually a compliment.

Many people are very slick, but they are also very artificial. They're simply not natural – not themselves. This is true of many politicians. They pretend to speak with authority, but people ask themselves: 'What is actually behind what he/she is saying?' and 'Does it mean anything?'

I think some people who listen to my speeches expect me to be as smooth as a practised after-dinner speaker. But this is not the case. It's not the real world – and it's not the real me. Of course, I drop in occasional humorous stories; doing this helps to keep the audience interested. But I talk principally about the real issues we all have to cope with. How to overcome adversity and achieve your best from the natural resources you possess undoubtedly captivates most people.

One of the businessmen I most admire is Richard Branson, who, although he often appears as the figurehead for his Virgin empire, clearly doesn't relish public appearances. He recognized early on that the profile of his business was important, but – probably because he's quite shy – putting himself in front of the

be flexible

media in the way he does is probably a lot harder for him than people imagine.

When requests began arriving for me to make public appearances, I could have said: 'Sorry, public speaking's not for me' and 'I'm not a natural, so therefore I won't do it.' But I persevered. Nevertheless, I was realistic about what I could and couldn't achieve. This does require some fairly searching self-analysis. There is more about dealing with negativity, your greatest potential enemy, in Chapter 8.

be aware of your capabilities

Everyone has different skills and abilities, and the important thing is to know what yours are and be flexible enough to see how they can be used in different ways.

CASE STUDY

Robert (44)

Married with three children, Robert has a degree in economics and a fairly well-paid job in the City, but desperately wants to get out of the daily commuter routine and have his own business. He wants to run a tax consultancy for self-employed people and small firms because he's read this is an expanding part of the economy.

be flexible

First he must go through the steps discussed earlier in this book. He must ask himself:
- Have I really thought through my goal?
- Is my family as enthusiastic as I am?
- Can we afford a reduction in income in the short term, and the domestic upheaval this may entail?
- What if things don't work out as planned? Will I be able to adapt to the situation and consider another area of self-employment?
- If the worst comes to the worst, could I find a job similar to the one I'm planning to leave?

Robert needs to write down: 'By the end of [date] I will have [number] clients and will have an annual income/turnover of at least [amount].' This, if you like, is his gold standard. It is where he needs to be in say, three years. But he needs to adhere to it.

Then he needs to work backwards, and set himself similar targets in maybe six months, and one and two years.

Finally, he must ask himself what he must do to achieve his aim:
- What stages do I need to go through?
- Will I need to attend evening classes to acquire new skills?
- How will I acquire clients and attract business?

Adopting a careful and meticulous approach will give Robert a good chance of success in his chosen endeavour.

be flexible

Now let's look at another example.

> **CASE STUDY**
>
> ### Clare (30)
>
> Although a successful social worker, Clare dreams of joining the legal profession. She has had some dealings in this area and finds it fascinating, and it will almost certainly be more lucrative than her present job.
>
> Her dream may be to become a lawyer, but the realism discussed earlier warns her that she may be over-ambitious, maybe not. If she sets out with lofty aims, and the horizon appears too distant, the danger is that she will soon begin to feel disillusioned and start using demotivating statements, such as: 'I'll never achieve that' and, in some cases, 'I'm not good enough'.
>
> It's better for her to approach her aim in achievable stages. Apart from any other consideration, the satisfaction she gains from reaching each level will sustain her enthusiasm.
>
> Her first step would almost certainly be to gain a degree in law. This is essential. In the meantime, it would be unwise to jettison her existing career, even if she could afford to do so. The preferable route could therefore be to consider a part-time or Open University course. Once she had completed this, she could look at specializing and moving on to the next stage. She might then realize that her initial dream of becoming a lawyer is unattainable, but that other work has begun to interest her – maybe some area that involves her existing work and legal processes.

> Clare must keep in mind that she wants to improve herself, but that this doesn't mean locking herself into such a narrow structure that her original goal becomes non-negotiable. She must be precise in her aims, but keep her options open. In essence, she must be prepared to be flexible.

how flexible are you?

You are in business with an associate, someone you have known for years. You have grown up together. The company is performing well enough but, you feel, not to its full potential. You recognize that your friend lacks imagination and is fearful about what may happen if the company expands. What do you do?

- Tell him frankly that it is best you go your separate ways.
- Continue as you are. Friendship is more important than maximizing profits.
- Discuss your concerns. Suggest that you take more control of the business.
- Discuss your concerns. Suggest that your friend concentrates on a specific role that appears to suit him, while you take more control of the business.
- Plan the formation of a separate company over which you have full control.

be flexible

Any or all of these options may be the correct one. Without knowing the precise context and details of the company, it is impossible to say. What is important is that you take stock, examine the deficiencies in the company, look at your priorities, and take action.

stay on top in the workplace

Favourites aren't found only in sport. They are found in the workplace too: people who are expected to come out on top and stay there. Just as on the sports field, it is usually no coincidence if it is always the same person who dominates in a company. It is not just fate. I've been to a number of companies over the years to present sales awards, and I've returned to the same ones time after time. I've noticed that the presentation to the top salesperson will often go to the same person. Why does this happen?

'How does anyone keep increasing sales?' I asked myself. 'They've got to find new people to sell to all the time, and, depending on the field they're in, they're probably in a relatively defined area. If a company's product is, say, engines, it's likely that they can be sold only to a car or boat manufacturer. How do salespeople go on year in, year out, producing very good performances?

Top salespeople have to be focused, and their attitude to life is positive. If something goes wrong, they adapt, they are flexible, and they are very methodical. It's not just their talent in selling – though that's important. It's their skill in establishing goals and then organizing themselves to get the best out of their selling ability by structuring their lives a certain way. They plan all calls in advance, rather than just doing them ad hoc. It's possible to strike lucky every now and again, and have a good month or a good three months, even a good year. But to do it year in, year out, there has to be a precise, long-term strategy. On top of all this, it takes intensity and a lot of effort.

Redgrave's reminders

- ✔ In the real world things never go smoothly.
- ✔ Nothing is written in stone.
- ✔ Be prepared for the unexpected.
- ✔ Pressure can be good for you – it's a stepping-stone on the way to success.
- ✔ Be aware of your capabilities, and be prepared to adapt them.

CHAPTER 5

look ahead and stay ahead

REDGRAVE'S RULE:

PERFECT THE ART OF MENTAL REHEARSAL.

Elite athletes devote most of their time to physical training, so when they reach the Olympic Games, they find that all the participants are in pretty similar shape. In my sport, with coaches from the former East Germany spread around the world, the training is pretty much the same, too. Similarly, many people in business, the professions and creative industries, such as design and architecture, have the same kind of skills.

So what is the difference that will ensure one group of athletes crosses the line quicker than others, that a company is consistently successful, that an architectural practice maintains an international reputation? As stressed later, in Chapter 8, it's got to be the mental edge. Once you have the basics under control, you can use your mind to increase your percentage of doing well. This is where visualization, or mental rehearsal, is important.

Nowadays many sportsmen and women use visualization, though there are conflicting views about its benefits. One strong advocate is the Olympic gold medal-winning cyclist Chris Hoy. After his victory over Arnauld Tournant by 185 thousandths of a second, in the 1-km time trial at Athens, he admitted: 'It's weird. I've spent so many hours training and thinking about it. It's such a lifetime's ambition. I knew I'd won, but I couldn't absorb it. That's why I didn't start punching the air. I was just riding around. I do a lot of visualization, where you go through your rides mentally in advance. It went so exactly like I'd rehearsed it, I thought it wasn't real. It took a while to realize that it was. It was kind of bizarre.'

I can appreciate what he means. It was out in Seoul before the 1988 Olympics that I first came across visualization techniques, although I had actually been using a form of visualization myself for years. I was introduced to the concept by Simon Holmes, the brother of my pairs partner, Andy, and the official psychologist to the British rowing team. Simon asked us to lie down and relax every part of the body in turn. It was a form of self-hypnosis, or ultra-deep concentration, where we had to turn off every other thought (as though the mind were equipped with a tap) and just concentrate on the elements we were going to confront during the race. I'd used that technique quite often, particularly during my spell of competitive bob-sleighing, when my mind was really buzzing during warm-up routines.

I discovered I could switch myself off completely, be totally focused on what I had to do, and mentally go through the process of a race. That's what visualization is all about. The 'what if' situation, I call it. You use your imagination to its full extent and project things forward. 'What if' this happens? 'What 'if' that happens? In business you could use the technique to decide between two alternative courses of action. Projecting the results of each into the future will allow you to decide which is the best option. It could also be applied to choosing between two job offers.

plan for contingencies

Visualizing wasn't just a procedure to put myself through immediately before a race. I had my own way of preparing for a major event. In the months and even years leading up to an Olympic final I would mentally rehearse that race. I'd do it in the most mundane of circumstances: pushing a trolley round a supermarket when doing the family shopping; on an airline flight; on a long drive.

I'd ask myself hundreds of questions: 'What would we do if the Australians did this at a certain stage, or the Italians did that at another point? What if we got off to a bad start? How would we respond to that? What if we feel we've made a really good start and yet we're not leading? How would we cope with that?' With an event as significant as the Olympics, I'd start imagining what could happen three or four years in advance. By the time the actual event came round, I'd have gone through the eventualities so many times in rehearsal that I'd be able to react to the real experiences automatically. To an extent, it was my way of dealing with nerves. I always got nervous just before a world championship final. With the Olympics, the nerves kicked in four years in advance.

If an event doesn't go the way you thought it would, or someone does something you're not expecting, you're faced with a challenge. That challenge may be daunting, but at least if you have visualized it in advance, you are initially prepared for it. If a challenge feels familiar you can try to do something about it, rather than panic.

visualize what could happen

Try thinking of visualization as a mental DVD playing in your mind, allowing you to see how events will unfold. You want to be in a situation where, whatever happens, your mind will be saying: 'I've been here before. I can deal with this.' In some sports there would be a lot of previous, similar experiences to draw on; in others, such as football, everything happens so quickly that you barely have time to think, so visualization is less relevant. Rowing falls into neither of these categories.

In my sport we rowed in a major final about five times a year, with the pinnacle – the Olympics – every four years. Even if we were going into an Olympic final as favourites because we'd won all our races up to that point, we'd still be talking about only 20 races in total. We therefore had to gain competition experience from somewhere else, and visualization is a good tool for doing that. We go through the race process in our heads hundreds of times because the more we go through it, the more answers we have to all the eventualities.

But how do you deal with the totally unexpected?

> **EXERCISE:** VISUALIZATION
>
> - Imagine that you've gone to the video store and picked out the film entitled *My Imagination*, placed it in your video machine and played it.
> - Close your eyes and allow the event, whatever it is, to play through your mind.
> - Imagine what problems you might come across, and work out what you would do.

expect the unexpected

It's one thing to predict what someone might do; it's quite another to respond if that person behaves in a totally unexpected way. It's therefore essential to be prepared and expected the unexpected. This is a concept that should be considered when you are preparing and planning your goals.

When Matthew Pinsent and I were rowing together or in a four we attempted to ensure that we never came off the water saying of our rivals: 'Hmm, we didn't expect them to do that.' Why didn't we expect them to do that? We should have prepared. In the build-up to a championship or the Olympics, Matthew and I used to rank the opposition, using every scrap of information available, including their current form. We'd give them stars, with five being allocated to the ones we rated very highly. By doing that, we produced an order in which they should finish (behind us).

At the end of this process we'd say: 'Well, that's how we've analysed it, but there's bound to be someone who will do something unusual. There'll be a surprise somewhere. Where's that surprise coming from?' We reckoned it would be either a crew who should perform highly and don't, or a crew less highly rated who somehow come in far better than anticipated. We used to look at every area to detect the potential source of a surprise and how it might manifest. We were looking for something more than the obvious. Whatever the circumstances, we didn't want to be thrown off our stroke. That, to me, was the professional approach.

It's the same in business. You may be confident that you're streets ahead of a rival, but that doesn't mean you can relax. Ask yourself what you would do if you were in his or her shoes. Think of all kinds of possibilities, then decide how you would cope with them. Mentally rehearse experiences, good or bad. Whatever situation you're in, you've got to be able to come up with a method of dealing with a threat.

But just a minute, you might interrupt. How can you do that if, by definition, you don't know what the unexpected is? That's a good question to which there are several answers:

- Be receptive; accept that you have more than one channel to go down.
- Decide on the areas where you could make improvements if you had to.
- Be prepared to adapt even your most cherished plans if necessary.
- Imagine that you are your competitor, and think what you would do if you were in their shoes.

look ahead and stay ahead

In our case, Matthew and I hoped to be able to follow our race plan, with all our rivals racing exactly as we had expected them to. But when racing against five other boats, the chances of someone doing something unanticipated were pretty high. In those circumstances, it was essential to think ahead.

maintain the will to win

Sometimes, ultimately, it was sheer bloody-minded doggedness that got us through. Remember, the final of the coxless fours at Athens? Everyone had anticipated an easy victory for Great Britain, yet when it came to the final 500 metres, Matthew Pinsent and his crew simply could not shake off the Canadians. They had planned for everything, and Matthew believed that 30 decisive strokes to 'empty the tank', as he graphically described that final effort by the British crew, would do the trick and leave them half a length up. It didn't. They were still slightly behind. In the end, brute determination got the British crew over the line first by a fraction of a second, 'with my last ebbs of energy', as Matthew put it. The truth was, though, that they were in a position to win because they had prepared for the unexpected. The fact that the British were the stronger and more talented crew ensured that they prevailed, albeit by the narrowest of margins. Jurgen Grobler, their coach, talked about the last stroke as the most important – the one that could win the race. How right he was.

Visualization is all about being able to foresee problems and rationalize them. It certainly worked for Team GB on Schinias

Lake outside Athens in 2004. However, I would stress that the technique can be applied at any time, not simply before major events. I used to employ it before training, or if there was an ergo (rowing machine) assessment.

stay one step ahead

Visualization, according to sports psychologists, is a very important tool for an athlete, but it can be applied equally well to other walks of life. There are two ways of achieving it:

1 Visualize yourself sitting in an armchair and watching yourself perform in an event. Like watching a TV programme, you are an outsider looking in.
2 Visualize actually being at the event and seeing yourself perform.

Experts say that it doesn't really matter which way you look at it, but I'd say that method 2 is what most people do. After all, they're the ones in their own minds who are actually standing on the rostrum receiving the medal, having achieved whatever they set out to do.

Can this concept of visualization assist us in everyday life? I believe it can in many ways. Life is all about being set a series of questions, even though much of the time we're not aware of it. The winner, assuming there are no other significant flaws, is the man or woman who comes prepared with most, if not all, of the answers.

There are occasions, say, at an examination or job interview, when you will have some idea of what the questions will be. On the

look ahead and stay ahead

other hand, there are many times when you won't. When this is the case, consider everything that might come your way. Don't be lost for answers. Consider the following scenarios.

Scenario 1
You have to give a presentation at work. It's not something you have done before, at least not to such a large audience of your peers – and the boss.

Imagine yourself as an actor going through rehearsal, but then swing away, like a television camera, and watch yourself, as though you are a member of the audience. What do you see? Do you see someone who is confident? Or someone who looks nervous, stressed and ill at ease? If it's the former, you can go to the meeting feeling relaxed and ready to give the presentation all you've got. If it's the latter, you still have time do something about it. Rehearse what you are going to say and how you say it, or do some relaxation exercises.

Scenario 2
You have an appointment with the boss, during which you intend to ask for a pay rise.

Although you might feel that the rise is totally justified, it is essential before you go in to borrow an idea from John F. Kennedy and think not what your company can do for you, but what you can do for your company. You have to sell yourself as a valuable, even invaluable, member of the workforce. Nobody got rich by selling themselves short.

Think beforehand what awkward questions you would ask if you were the boss…

- Why should he/she pay me more?
- What if they could recruit somebody younger, and with more energy, for less money, not more?
- What am I offering as an employee that makes me worth more?
- Do I honestly think I am worth extra?
- What is my reaction if the boss says no?

This last question is particularly crucial. Do you get angry? Bang your fist on the table? Do you threaten to quit? What would be the implications then? How would the boss react? Could he/she be bluffing? Would it be possible to call his/her bluff?

Let me give you a personal example of how rehearsing for an event can be useful. When I was a youngster of nine or ten at the local school, there was one boy bullying another. Although I was physically strong, I wasn't aggressive by any stretch of the imagination, but one day I stepped in and said, 'Leave him alone'. The bully was from a really tough family. I knew his older brother had been in borstal, as detention centres were called then. The bully's response was to say, 'Right, I'll see you after school.'

If we'd got into a fight there and then, I'm not sure what I would have done. For the rest of the day I knew it was going to happen, and though I must admit I was scared as I thought about it, I went through in my own mind how I would deal with the situation. Well, we had our fight: his face was cut up and his nose was bleeding,

look ahead and stay ahead

and he went running off – to get his brother, or so I thought, but he actually ran to my mother because we lived nearly next door to the school. She cleaned him up and took him back to his parents. Fortunately, they said: 'You got what you deserved. You went out this morning saying you were going to get Steve Redgrave.' He'd obviously been planning a showdown. In the event, I taught him a lesson and even got respect from his brother, too.

The important point here is that I was prepared for what was coming up. Mentally, I was ready for it, although I'd never really been in a fight in my life. Although it was a relatively trivial incident, I had built it up as a big event in my mind. It was the equivalent, later in life, of a major rowing final.

prepare yourself for stress

I've competed at five Olympics and raced in six finals. Having been through those experiences, I know what an ordeal the build-up can be. I also appreciate how this happens in business life. Waiting for a meeting or preparing to give a presentation can be equally daunting in their own way. Similarly, anxiety can build up when you are doing something for the first time – taking a holiday alone, for example, or starting a new job.

However, there are ways of overcoming that anxiety and stress, as I told Daniel Caines, the British athlete who was one of my Team Visa group. Daniel, who had been number one at 400 metres in Great Britain, and third in the International Association of Athletics

Federations rankings, had said to me before Athens: 'I was at the last Olympics and made the semi-finals in the 400 metres, and the final of the relay, where we came sixth. This time I'm going for a medal. What am I going to feel like the night before? How am I going to cope with that situation?'

The fact that he was thinking about that ahead of the Athens Games, focusing on his own performance and preparation, impressed me. However, it was not an easy question to answer. It's one thing to visualize tactics and how you see the race developing. It's difficult to visualize how you're going to feel about the sitting around and waiting – the mental preparation.

It would have been unhelpful to say: 'Oh, just chill out. Don't worry about it.' And equally unhelpful to say: 'It's really difficult.' Instead, I told him about my own experiences. I told him how, at the Sydney Olympics in 2000, Matthew and I were sharing a room that had no curtains and overlooked the Olympic stadium. In our vision, as we tried to get to sleep on the eve of our coxless fours final, was the Olympic flame, fluttering in the distance. That was enough to inspire us. Admittedly, emotions were running pretty high, so I dozed, rather than got a good night's sleep, but the following day we won our race.

Stress is inevitable before an Olympics final. Most athletes have the chance of going to only one Olympics, maybe two. Few have done more. In rowing the competition is the biggest event you can do, with precious little competition in between. We therefore spend the periods between races, sometimes several months, trying to make sure we get things right. If we get them wrong, we have a long time to live with it, which makes it all the more stressful.

look ahead and stay ahead

I can remember waiting for finals many times, at both Olympics and world championships, and thinking: 'What on earth am I doing here? This is a nightmare, yet I still come back and do it again. Why am I doing this? I've done 12 months' training for this event; now I'm sitting here scared about going out and competing.' You can prepare for your warm-up and your race, but it's really difficult to prepare for the waiting around. We talk about the pain of training and racing, but it's nothing compared with waiting for the race to happen.

As you work through your strategy towards your goal, you may undergo the same kind of stress. See below for some suggestions on how to handle it.

WAYS TO DEAL WITH STRESS

- Think about how far you've come towards achieving your goal.
- List the problems you've already encountered – and overcome.
- Concentrate on the efforts you've already put into realizing your dream, and tell yourself it's not worth letting them go to waste.
- Tell yourself that all you can do is your best and that walking away would certainly be failure.
- Look back on the occasions when you've succeeded in doing what you set out to do.
- Stop thinking about how stressed you are; instead, visualize yourself achieving your goal.

I was determined not to let my nerves get to me. I used to tell myself that it would be a waste of a year – or four years – if I didn't go out and put in my best performance: win, lose or draw. To lose a race having underachieved is difficult to take; losing when you have put in your best effort is even tougher, but you can be satisfied you have done your best.

deal with expectations

Probably the worst stress situation I've experienced was at Atlanta in 1996, when media interest in rowing suddenly exploded. Gone were the days of casual contact with about 25 interested journalists. Now we were in the midst of a media frenzy, being followed at virtually every training session, and with about 250 journalists at our first race.

During the build-up at our training camps in Europe and Canada we had been isolated for about six weeks, and found the motivation quite easy and straightforward. However, the closer we got to the event, the more expectations were heaped on our performance. The press conference we had to face after our first race was quite a shock; we had to deal with the world's expectations as well as our own.

Matthew and I simply said that on 27 July we were going out to win an Olympic gold medal, just as we had done at Barcelona. Having said this, however, we started playing it in our minds and thinking: 'Actually, this thing is a hell of a lot bigger than it should be.' Our usual habit was to play down the big events, but this one had been built so high, a long time in advance that, once we got there, there was no relief. It was a huge media event, with intense public interest, and extremely tough to cope with.

There were certain times in those last ten days when I could see myself blowing it. I'd say to myself: 'I can't cope with this. There's no way I'll be able to get a good performance out of myself.' In simple terms, didn't feel entirely in control of the emotions I was going through.

This was where visualization came in. I'd see myself racing against the Australians, our principal opponents, thinking at 500 metres: 'We're level', at 1000 metres: 'We're drawing ahead', then coming into the last 500 metres and seeing myself look across at them and thinking: 'There's no way they're going to beat us.'

When you're stressed out by the thought of having to meet other people's expectations as well as your own, the solution is to get back to the positives. In our case, we had done the training and preparation, were confident of our boat speed, and we knew what we were capable of. We'd had four years of not losing a race. Why should we lose this one? OK, the Australian crew was one we'd never raced before, but they couldn't be that much better than the guys we'd competed against. They were good, but we always felt we could beat them.

control the controllables

When you feel that events are running away with you, it's essential to pull yourself back and control what can be controlled. That's what sports psychologists talk about, and the same thing holds true in all walks of life. It's important that you don't become obsessed with areas you can't influence. If there's a downturn in the economy, for example, there's not much you can do about it. What you can do is make sure your company's products are head and shoulders above those of your rivals, and thus ensure that they are the ones customers will buy. In sport, what is the point of worrying about weather conditions, for example, when they're something you can't control? Instead, be realistic and take control of the situations over which you do have some influence.

Following this philosophy enabled me to conquer my demons during the Atlanta Olympics in 1996, when there had been all manner of distractions, including the bomb blast in Centennial Park that killed one person. At one stage, I contemplated not racing at all. It just didn't seem right for Matthew Pinsent and me to take part in our final under those circumstances. But then I focused hard and said to myself: 'Well, if we don't race, another crew will become Olympic champions. What will that have achieved?'

That was an extreme situation of course, but it's right to question yourself when the doubts appear. Ask: 'Why am I doing this? How important is this to me?', and use visualization to answer, 'How good am I going to feel when I have achieved this?'

look ahead and stay ahead

Four years on from Atlanta, I honestly felt that Sydney would probably be my last Olympics, and I wanted to make sure I enjoyed the experience. I said to myself: 'This is probably going to be the last time. Enjoy the moment.' As far as the rowing management was concerned, I wasn't in race mode. From the outside, I appeared too concerned with the enjoyment factor and not the seriousness of what we were trying to do. It was not until a day and a half before the final that I turned into my normal miserable self – showing the side of me that always appeared when getting ready to race.

With a fifth gold medal at stake, people thought I was under more pressure than at Atlanta, and it might have seemed that way from the outside. I knew there'd be enormous interest in what I and we as a four were trying to do. But this time, even though media attention was intense, I didn't allow it to affect me in the same way as at the Atlanta Games. I felt much more in control of the situation.

The lesson to be learnt from my experience is the importance of focus. But for heaven's sake enjoy yourself, whatever goal you're fixed on.

take time off and think ahead

If you are seriously stressed, I see no harm in taking time off to think about the future. I am always amused by a story my wife Ann tells on this subject, although it has a serious point to it. She says: 'When I was in medical school, 20-odd years ago, there was a "mad" cardiologist who treated stressed-out top executives by putting them in bed for a month. I saw them as I went round the wards during my student days.

'He simply took people who had displayed some cardiac symptoms, removed them from their stressful situation, let their body calm down, then allowed them back to work again. He would do that rather than put them on drugs. And it worked. Their performance improved greatly.

'It was very radical treatment for the time. He'd talk to them beforehand, advise them what they needed to do, but they wouldn't do it. So, to his way of thinking, the only alternative was to hospitalize them.'

For most people, this would be rather too radical a way of taking time off. But the basic concept is a valid one. Put your immediate problems to the back of your mind and concentrate on thinking about the future. Remember, almost anything can be achieved if you prepare adequately and take things one step at a time.

A good example of preparation is the story of how football managers would tell their players to clean their boots the night before a game. The boots might not have needed cleaning, but that was irrelevant. The managers were simply stimulating their players' mental processes and getting them to start thinking about the match. For me, this is the equivalent of visualizing an Olympic final as I walk around a supermarket.

Redgrave's reminders

✔ Turn your mind into a mental DVD player.
✔ Expect the unexpected to happen.
✔ Stay one step ahead – don't be lost for answers.
✔ Be prepared to deal with stress.
✔ Control what can be controlled.

CHAPTER 6

train to win

REDGRAVE'S RULE:

' THERE'S NO SUBSTITUTE FOR PUTTING IN THE WORK. '

This chapter is about the hard work – or in my rowing career, the training – that is necessary to make your dreams come alive. No, don't turn the page: hard work is the necessary evil. It has to be done to make it all happen. You can't be successful if you don't put in the work, the dedication and the commitment.

Flair, talent or natural ability is only part of the answer. If you have the ability and don't put in the hard work, yes, you can achieve a certain amount, but you can achieve greater things if you blend these elements together. Being able to perform once to the standard you desire is important; but achieving it once means that you should be able to do it again. It's all about creating consistent performances.

Some people train to win. I used to train to eliminate the possibility of defeat. It's just looking at it from a slightly different perspective. Instead of focusing on trying to win, I concentrated on not making mistakes, on refusing to entertain failure.

When Matthew Pinsent and I rowed as a pair, we felt that we were the best in the world. This wasn't just because we had won a certain championship or event, but because we would be ready to race at any time. 'Just tell us when a particular race is going to be staged and we'll be ready.' That was our philosophy.

'You want to race next week? We'll still beat you because we train at such a high level all the time.' We wouldn't accept anything below this standard.

stay focused all the time

The truth in sport and in business is that if you're intent on remaining at the top in these ultra-competitive times, you have to maintain a highly focused regime. And even this may not be sufficient, whatever your talent. That's why of all my contemporaries over last quarter century I'd say Pete Sampras was the supreme sportsman.

Why?

One of the questions I've been asked most often throughout my career is: 'Which sportsmen or women do you really admire?' I've never been one for hero-worshipping, but my answer is always simply this: 'I admire whoever extracts the best performances consistently from the abilities they have.' I'd say one of the people who fits this description is Pete Sampras – the man who included seven Wimbledon championships among his 14 grand slam titles because he invariably got the best out of himself. Most tennis aficionados would agree that Pete wasn't the most graceful or natural tennis player around. But – and this is the crucial factor – he had assets in many different areas, and by combining them consistently produced the optimum from what he had.

In a different sport entirely – snooker – Stephen Hendry is another player with phenomenal talent, but he also exemplifies the sportsman who doesn't leave things to chance. By contrast, George Best had all the natural ability anyone could desire, but never truly fulfilled himself. He achieved a great amount certainly; there were moments of supreme brilliance. Yet ultimately, he wasted his talent. That's a little harsh, you may be thinking. George played at the highest level – for Manchester United in their prime. How many footballers make it that far? Well, admittedly, there were circumstances that conspired against him. He was part of a Northern Ireland team that was always going to find it difficult to secure a place on the world stage. In his era they never qualified for a World Cup.

But this is not why George failed to fufil his potential. He failed because he had all the assets, but never got the best out of himself. He may have thrilled a lot of people, and certainly there will have been youngsters who thought, 'I wish I had just some of his gifts', but it would have been better had they contemplated what George *could* have done. He achieved what he did despite himself; he had the benefit of being at a great football club, under a legendary manager, the late Sir Matt Busby, where his talent was nurtured and his off-field extravagances were largely indulged. But he was an exception. As a rule, sporting giants are partly born and partly created – by their own commitment, as well as that of others, such as coaches, around them.

This is why when people say to me, as they often do, 'Sheer talent will get you to the top eventually, won't it? Surely it can't fail to do so?' I correct that notion. It is not true. Indeed, it is usually far from the case. Cream doesn't always rise to the top. Keep that in mind as you move on to the next stage.

set your training regime

You have your dream, you know it's realistic, you've established your goals and you've set out your strategy. But if you don't go out and make it happen, you won't get any further.

For me as an oarsman, making it happen meant ploughing up and down the river and doing the training for well over 20 years. In business if you don't pick up the phone and sell your project to somebody, and if you don't sit down and calculate the profit margins on those sales, you won't have a very successful business. If your dream is to be a top-class mountain climber, you'll need to start by walking just a little further every day and hiking up hills before you can tackle high peaks.

Yet people still say to me: 'Come on, Steve. What's the secret formula? What's the one thing that's going to make the difference?' Unfortunately, there is no one thing. There's no magic potion that will transform an average performer into a champion; if there were, I'd have bottled it myself. Everything rests on your own determination and application. Certainly, I would never have achieved what I have if I'd left my career in the hands of fate, simply believed in my talent and hadn't taken some radical decisions about my future.

But there are ways of making hard work if not fun, then at least an incentive, whether you're revising for exams, training for a sport or working long hours in the office.

discipline or routine?

The word 'discipline' crops up regularly in sport and business, and, indeed, in people's personal lives. Quitting smoking or losing weight are all about discipline, aren't they? Perhaps not.

Let me explain. Everyone regarded me as a very disciplined sportsman. I never saw myself as that. What I did see was someone who accepted and worked well with a routine – the routine of getting the work done. Routine is a boring little word, but it could be crucial to your success. It's routine that gets the bulk of the work done – the necessary work. The only discipline involved is that of turning up for training or to work because other people are relying on you.

A good illustration of the difference between discipline and routine arose when I had four months off after the Atlanta Olympics. During that time I used to take my daughter Natalie and a friend of hers to school. However, I was so used to driving along that road at about that time every morning when I was preparing for the Games that I often found myself driving automatically towards Henley, where I used to train, rather than heading for the school. I was following my old routine. It was routine that got me out of bed each morning at a certain time, not discipline. Discipline comes into it only when you are tempted to break your routine.

When I was rowing I used occasionally to break my routine by attending a function midway through the day, maybe to give a talk or presentation. It meant a break in training. If the event was in London, afterwards I'd have to drive near my Marlow home to return to Henley, where I'd make up afterwards for the training I'd missed by doing some on my own, maybe on the weights.

If I didn't go back, I wasn't letting anyone else down, only myself. So I'd be tempted to say: 'What's the point of going back? Missing one session isn't going to make any difference to our performance in Sydney [or whatever the goal was at that particular time].' Well, no. In the great scheme of things it probably wouldn't have made any difference at all. But if I had allowed myself to miss one session, it would have been easier to miss a second one, then a third and a fourth. Things would have spiralled out of control. Without realizing it, I would not be doing the work I was supposed to be doing. This is where discipline came in.

It's own-up time, and I have to confess I didn't always go back and do the training, even though I kidded Jurgen that I had. If things hadn't gone well, if we hadn't got the results we wanted, I'd have had to hold my hand up and say: 'It was probably my fault.' Of course, nobody else knew when I missed out on training. Just me. This is where being true to yourself, being realistic with yourself, comes in.

It is important to retain a balance. Sometimes you may need to change your routine to break the monotony. Doing this can refresh you, invigorate you – as long as your routine does not suffer over the long term. This can be as true in the workplace, or when preparing for a marathon, as it was for me.

> **SET ACHIEVABLE TRAINING GOALS**
>
> Don't set yourself objectives that you'll be unable to achieve. If you want to exercise as part of a weight-loss programme, decide to walk for 20 minutes a day rather than aiming for three hour-long sessions a week in the gym. If your plan is to broaden your client base at work, aim to contact one potential new customer a week rather than one a day. And remember: if you fail to keep to your routine, be honest with yourself – if no one else – about your failure.

routine is a positive force

The word 'routine' implies something so repetitive that it becomes instinctive. Routine is vital to the strategy you employ to reach your target. It is a positive force. During my career, the training was tough, relentless and certainly hard going. I got through the work, but, as I've already stressed, this was not because I was a disciplined athlete. I wasn't. Believe me, it would have been easier not to do the work than to complete it.

On a day-to-day basis, getting into a routine made the process much more acceptable. We were able to complete our training without thinking about it, although we obviously concerned ourselves with its quality and other elements within it. The same holds true in the workplace. If you are a salesman, you plan your day and make your calls. That's routine, not discipline.

I used to set my alarm clock before an early-morning outing. Was that being disciplined? It wasn't. It was routine. The discipline came when the alarm went off and I had to do something about it. It was my response to the alarm, not the action of setting it.

stay on track

There will be times when the going gets tough, when self-doubt creeps in, when it's simpler to take the easy option. When your mind says: 'I don't think I'll bother today. I'll leave it until tomorrow. I'm not going out on that 10-km run. I won't stick to my diet.' Again, it's time to be honest with yourself. Go back to basics. Have a discussion with yourself, if you like. Ask yourself: 'Why am I actually doing this?'

You may need to do more than that. Sometimes even winners have to resharpen their competitive edge and remind themselves just why they started a process in the first place. Here are some suggestions on what to do if this happens to you.

- List your reasons to be cheerful.
- Promise yourself a reward if you get through the day or the week.
- Think optimistically. What will be the long-term rewards when you achieve your aim?

- If you're determined to lose 12 kg (2 stone), think about why you started in the first place. Was it to raise your self-esteem? Improve your health? Was it a question of vanity? To gain the approval of friends of same sex, of the opposite sex? To enhance your desirability?
- If you've changed your career, recall why you made that decision. Money? Status? Improvement in lifestyle? Were you simply bored with your existing work?
- Think through what first inspired you, then visualize how it will turn out. Do you really want to waste what you have achieved? To throw away the opportunity of improving your life?

reward yourself – you deserve it

Self-reward is a valid concept. Just as children may be offered a treat if they do well in their exams, there's no reason why you shouldn't offer yourself a reward if you achieve something. This is good psychology.

Of course, your desire to attain your ultimate goal is your principal motivation, but there's no harm in creating a 'reward-by-achievement' system for yourself. Maybe a meal out at one end of the reward scale for a short-term goal, and a holiday at the other when you achieve a longer-term aim. After all, you deserve it. When you draw up your action plan (see page 59) make sure you include rewards at various stages.

The reward system works for many people – even Olympic gold medallists. Before the 1994 world championships, when a train to win

lot of pressure was building up, Matthew Pinsent decided that if we won our final, he would reward himself by taking helicopter lessons. I knew this was a real incentive for him: he wanted to get his pilot's licence, and talked about it quite a lot. He was determined to get behind that joystick, even though he knew the procedure would be costly. He simply said to himself: 'If I win, I can justify it.'

This process is all part of setting goals, which are stepping-stones on the way to achieving your ultimate dream. However, not everyone needs tangible rewards. Some people are content to accept that each step is part of achieving their ultimate aim, but others – and there is no harm in this – need something more material to keep them stimulated.

BE PREPARED TO MAKE SACRIFICES

It is almost certain that you won't succeed without some hardship, some decline in the lifestyle with which you have become familiar. Whether it's giving up alcohol or certain foods in a bid to become healthier, or attending evening classes instead of enjoying nights out at the pub, sacrifice is unavoidable.

In my case, I had to make a major change to the way I had lived my teenage years. After recognizing that I was determined to be a champion in my chosen sport of rowing, I decided that it could not be achieved on a part time basis. This was not purely a matter of focus; it was because

> I had to put in the training required. I could not seriously hold down another job while doing that. I had to channel all my energies into rowing if I was to succeed. Apart from anything else, I knew this was how my foreign rivals approached rowing. I had to regard it as a full-time occupation, despite the fact that when I started out it was perceived as a strictly amateur sport, even at the elite level. At that time there was precious little sponsorship, and certainly none for someone who was just a youngster with potential.

maximize your fitness

Getting fit may well be one of your goals, an end in itself. If not, it's essential that you're in good condition when you set out to achieve your dreams. This doesn't mean being able to run a four-minute mile, but it does mean having a body that can accept the physical and mental stresses that lie ahead. There's a straightforward reason for this. My wife Ann, an orthopaedic physician, who was team doctor to the Great Britain rowing squad, says: 'The principal aim is to maintain your cardiovascular – respiratory systems, or, to put it in more basic terms, ensure that your heart and lungs are operating efficiently. When you keep fit you stimulate the blood supply, and that fuels all the organs. A lot of people have heart failure because they're not using the body's most important muscle properly. The blood simply isn't pumping sufficiently, and it's not vitalizing all the organs essential for maintaining a healthy life. If you're a couch potato, the outcome will be a decline in the way your body operates – not what you want when you have to be at your best to achieve your goals.'

It's also important to remember that most people don't do the physical tasks their forefathers did, domestically or in the workplace, so they are not as fit. As Ann says: 'Because of technology, even at work we don't walk to see people. We email them. General levels of fitness are getting lower. Kids do less at school.'

So whether you are planning a keep-fit campaign for its own benefits or in association with another, separate goal, you will have to make a serious declaration: 'I am going to change my lifestyle fundamentally.' It's no good embarking on your campaign for five weeks, then going back to your previous way of life. The same applies if you are trying to lose weight.

Ann's long-term goal was to run the London Marathon with me in 2001, and she remembers how difficult she found the training at first, despite having been an excellent rower in her younger years: 'When I first started training, after the birth of our third child, Zak, in 1998, I got from the bottom of our road to the bottom of the next road. That's as far as I could run. A friend and I ran together. We'd get sick, we'd get sore and we'd get out of breath. But we built it up from there, gradually, until we achieved our goal.'

ANN'S ADVICE FOR MAXIMUM FITNESS

- Start at the level that is appropriate to you. All too often, people go to a gym and are given a programme, but they've never done any gym work before. The result is that they become disillusioned or, worse still, go at it gung-ho and end up hurting themselves.
- Find an exercise programme that's realistic, that will fit into your life and routine. Fitness can be improved by making incredibly basic changes.
- Start off by just walking – 15 minutes a day is better than nothing. Walking helps to develop the exercise habit.
- Make exercise fun. It might be tough going at times, or there would be no point in doing it, but it's important to enjoy whatever activity you choose. If you can't stand racket sports or going into a gym, don't do it. Find something else, that you will continue.
- Remember: no matter how determined you are, you are not the person you were 20 or 30 years ago. Trying to get back to the level you were at then is not possible.
- Build up gradually to a stage where you can consider a more ambitious form of exercise. Formulate your plan of how to achieve this, perhaps on a reward-for-results basis.
- Do not exercise until it hurts. Get to the point where it feels uncomfortable, then stop. Next time you'll be able to go further.

For most people, exercising on a regular basis means their output increases: they are more alert and get more done. Often the first step – getting off the couch – is the most difficult. After that, because exercise improves the blood supply and produces endorphins (chemicals that give a feeling of well-being), people start to feel better.

Ann tells a story that will strike a chord with many people. 'During the course of my work I was treating a female patient who suffered from a bad hip. She could barely walk, let alone do anything more active, but one day she asked me: "Do you think I could run?" I said: "Yes, but do it very gently. A bit at a time." Eventually, after a few months, she could run 5 km (3 miles). It may not sound that much, but it was a significant personal victory for her.

'I'd say the same to anyone. If five minutes is all you can do at first, then do five minutes. Once this becomes easy, build it up. It will take time, and you will need to work at it. Make what you are trying to achieve realistic and incremental.'

What Ann says about build-up is very true. This is why my first three training sessions (say, to run the London Marathon) after six months off are unpleasant. I tend to do too much. I try to get back immediately to what I used to do when I was fit. I think: 'Well, I should be able to run for 20 minutes, half an hour, whatever.' If I run for 20 minutes, it's my heart and lungs that are the problem, rather than stiffness. I probably do too much to start with.

However, I know that once I've trained three or four times, it gets easier. Although each run is difficult, I progress each time.

give as much as you've got – no more

Do some set exercise regularly, every day or every other day, and remember: stop when it hurts. If you keep pushing through the pain barrier, you condition your brain to think 'exercise hurts'. As a result, when you have the opportunity not to exercise, you don't. If there is no pain, the brain receives a good message: 'Hey, this feels good; it's not a hardship.'

It's different for superfit athletes. They don't think about pain – it's not an issue. I was always amazed at how obsessed journalists were with it. 'How are you going to feel after 500 metres?' they'd ask. Yes, there is pain, but you're physically and mentally prepared; you're conditioned for the race. The pain will be unbearable only if you're not in the right condition, or ill, or if there's another outside factor. When you're rowing in an Olympic final you're geared up to give a certain performance. If you're not winning, you try to push it that little bit more to get in front, but you've only got a certain capacity. You can't give any more than you've got.

People often ask: 'Where should I start in my exercise regime? Which activity would you suggest?' I run because I find it easy. I can just open the door and go. However, in truth, running and jogging are not necessarily the best forms of exercise because they cause wear and tear on the knee joints – especially if someone is overweight. For more on running and other alternatives see page 132, overleaf.

train to win

EXERCISE REGIMES

Cycling: A good activity, but it depends on whether you're carrying any injuries. Obviously, if you have back problems, you shouldn't get on a bike.

Running: You don't have to belong to a club or need specialist equipment; just a pair of training shoes. You should probably do no more than 15 minutes a day, and you may have to build up to that.

Stretching: Something as simple as stretching is an excellent way to start your fitness regime. It won't help your cardiovascular-respiratory system, but it will help to strengthen your muscles.

Swimming: This is ideal (particularly for anyone who is overweight) because your weight is supported. But for the same reason it's very easy to overdo it. Swimming 20 lengths of a 25-metre (28-yard) pool is roughly equivalent to running a mile.

Walking: One of the best, and easiest, ways to exercise. If you need the motivation to get out there, you could consider buying a dog. You'd have to walk it, wouldn't you? A lot of people I know enjoy that. Their excuse is that it's for the dog's benefit, not theirs. No matter what weather is, they've got to go out twice a day.

Maybe in time we will evolve into animals that maintain low cholesterol and stay reasonably healthy without much exercise. People like that will be the survivors. Until that happens… we have to deal with the bodies we have. They aren't designed to cope with many of the physical activities we attempt.

Now, with all this in mind, you can write your plan of action. Here are the goals of a former Olympic rower in his early forties, a diabetic, who has suffered from colitis, who wishes to maintain his health and fitness in retirement:

1 Maintain a weight of _____ or less.
2 Ensure that, as a diabetic, his blood-sugar level remains within a range of _____ and _____ (in other words, tightly controlled).
3 Run at least _____ times a week for _____ minutes.
4 Long-term goal: complete the London Marathon in less than 4 hours 55 minutes (his time in 2001).

Redgrave's reminders

✔ Hard work is the necessary evil if you want to win at life.
✔ Cream doesn't necessarily rise to the top.
✔ Learn to love routine, not despise it.
✔ Reward yourself when you achieve a training goal – you deserve it.
✔ Exercise must be fun.

CHAPTER 7

learn from the experts

REDGRAVE'S RULE:

YOU CAN'T LEAVE TALENT TO CHANCE

Once you have decided on your goals and have planned your overall strategy, you will undoubtedly receive advice, some of it asked for, some of it not, and some of it probably unwanted.

Don't be afraid to learn and seek inspiration from others. Of course, if you are renovating your own house, advice from a builder or decorator will be invaluable; you don't have to take advice only from others in your own field of interest. If you are a sportsman or woman, a coach in a discipline other than yours could tell you a lot about how to be focused; someone in business might have a special expertise – administration, for example – that will help you if you are trying to cope with a growing company in the creative industry. But don't just copy others: adapt their ideas for your own use.

Remember, it's much easier to follow someone else's lead than break new ground yourself. I never had that advantage. I had to make my own way in a sport that wasn't spectacularly successful at international level. I did it by refusing to accept the status quo that existed at the time. It wasn't in my nature to accept second best. I realized that I wasn't going to be the champion that I was determined to become if I followed only the methods we employed in the United Kingdom. I therefore made a point of looking at methods used abroad, particularly in the Eastern Bloc, and in other sports.

do your homework

I learnt the hard way that success doesn't just happen by itself. Having been coached in my early years by Francis Smith, a teacher at my secondary school, I subsequently went under the wing of Mike Spracklen, who is still an international coach. He was responsible for the Canadian crew who came so close to thwarting the gold expectations of the Great Britain four at Athens. Back then, at the age of 21, I believed I possessed the ability, and thought that if I bided my time, success would happen. It was just a question of when it was going to be.

It was perhaps fortunate, in terms of my long-term career, that I was well beaten in the world championships of 1983. (At that time, I was single sculling, which involves using two oars rather than one.) That defeat forced me to look at things differently. It sounds crazy to say it now, but if I'd carried on as previously, I'd never have won the world championships, let alone Olympic gold medals. What happened was that Mike Spracklen and I used the defeat as a springboard to learn from other sports disciplines as well as rowing, and looked closely at the methods used elsewhere in the world.

This strategy can be applied to anyone determined to achieve a particular goal, but it's surprising how many people don't do their

learn from the experts

homework. It sounds ridiculously obvious, but if you're planning to run a marathon, speak to somebody who's completed one. Read about people who've participated, and learn about possible pitfalls. The same is true in business. Learn not just from other people's successes, but from their mistakes. If you're planning to invest your savings in opening a restaurant, talk to people who've tried and failed, as well as to those who have succeeded.

Striving for a goal is like going into battle, and expert knowledge will be a crucial part of your armoury. With so much information on the Internet, as well as in books, there is no excuse for not possessing sufficient background knowledge.

The point I am making is that you should not be afraid of learning – from any source.

learn from what other people do

In the early days I was aware I had a talent, and was determined to use it as best I could. Yet I also knew that to be really successful for a long period of time I had to look at things more deeply than that. You can't just turn up at a venue and use sheer talent to win. You might be able to do that once or twice, but not consistently. When I first started out it did not take long to develop into a top-class rower in the UK. In international competition, however, it was a different matter.

In order to become the champion that I was determined to be, I started by asking myself questions: 'Why are we doing things this way?' and 'Is this really the most efficient way?' I began to realize something important: the old ways aren't necessarily the best. In 1983 I started looking at what other sportsmen and women were doing. I knew there were elements missing from my performances, but I couldn't place what they were.

Mike Spracklen was a great analyser of things – one of the great thinkers in the sport. He'd lie awake at night pondering the problems. Sometimes he would mull over them for weeks, but he'd always come back with an idea. One of these ideas was to look at other sports. In particular, we looked at the way swimmers trained and tried to relate it to our sport to see what we could get out of it.

Swimming requires briefer stretches of effort than rowing: 2–4 minutes to cover 200–400 metres (220–440 yards), rather than the six minutes that we take, but the volume of training involved is immense. During steady-state training, swimmers plough up and down swimming lanes at a steady rate for mile after mile. Even the 100-metre swimmers do a huge amount of endurance work – just up and down, boring and tedious, but effective.

All reports from the Eastern Bloc countries suggested that they were training rowers in a way similar to our swimmers – steady-state sessions at really low rates. Without getting over-technical, the rate is the number of strokes an oarsman makes a minute. We'd heard that the top Russian pair, the Pimenov twins, Yuri and Nikolai, were rating 18 strokes a minute in their endurance training. We thought that was nonsense. What could be the advantage of training at a rate that was less than half of what I would probably be doing at the finish of a race?

learn from the experts

Even when Andy Holmes, my Olympic partner in 1988, and I were just 'out for a paddle', as we called it, a light workout, we were rating 24 strokes per minute. We never did anything less than that. All our training focus had been on doing explosive pieces of work for very short periods of time, with a rest in between. In those days we'd come off the water feeling that we simply couldn't do another stroke.

So with Mike, we learnt from the East Europeans and started doing training sessions that were longer and more endurance-based – in other words, based on stamina rather than speed. However, we still used to work very hard. That's why I made a very quick jump from being under the level for international competition to being on level, then above it.

be prepared to adapt

Later in my career, when Jurgen Grobler became Great Britain's head rowing coach in the early 1990s, he made me realize that there were other ways of looking at training.

Jurgen and I developed great mutual respect, but it was tough at first. I had to make a conscious effort to begin with to adapt to his East German system of training. Could his methods work here? I decided: 'Right, I'm ready to commit myself and give it my best shot to see if I can win another gold medal [having already won two]. The first year, I'll do what Jurgen says and follow his methods to the letter. If they work, fair enough. If not, I'll have to reconsider whether I want to continue with him.' It was exactly like the situation faced (rather more frequently) by a professional footballer coping with new management: adapt or move on.

The principal change Jurgen made to our routine was to insist that rates were reduced. Each stroke was vitally important, he insisted; you should not waste any individual stroke; it was the length and power that were important and that gave you the opportunity for rest. This scientific approach to training was vitally important as it gave greater consistency in results. Matthew Pinsent and I (who were then in the pair together) could not have succeeded without it.

This information is not intended just for those with an interest in rowing. I believe you can adapt it to whatever situation you are in. In business, for example, a steady-state approach is, in the long term, preferable to doing everything at top speed because that leads to burn-out. That's not to say you won't have to put in that extra spurt of energy occasionally – when you're preparing a sales pitch for a new client, for example. But ultimately, a structured, steady approach will win out.

I learnt a lot from Jurgen about my own particular area of interest, but it is important that you actively search for ideas, even outside your own domain. However, whether you're in sport or business, never simply steal other people's ideas. Mould them to your own design, adapting and improving them to benefit your needs. This is an important point, and one that is illustrated by my involvement with the now aborted UK Sports Institute.

THE UK SPORTS INSTITUTE

After I retired from rowing, I was invited on to the board of the UK Sports Institute (UKSI) by Sir Rodney Walker. It was a project conceived originally by the Conservative government under John Major, following the poor British showing at the Atlanta Olympics in 1996. The board's brief was to oversee the creation of a sports institute based on a much-acclaimed Australian model.

I went into it in a thoroughly idealistic mood, hopeful that we would have a blank piece of paper on which we could create a dream – an organization full of fresh ideas that would provide sporting success for Britain. I soon became disillusioned however, just as my fellow board member Steve Cram told me he had: 'I remember that I came out of sport full of big ideas and passion too, but eventually they'll grind you down.' After three or four meetings, I got totally fed up with the whole thing. There were too many hidden agendas, and eventually the idea died.

That said, I was never convinced that a straight copy of the Australian project was the right way to go. My argument, and this is my principle in life generally, is that ideas should be adapted to specific conditions. In the case of the proposed UK Sports Institute, I felt there should be centres of sporting excellence *throughout* the country, where resources would be concentrated for particular sports.

It is a debate that will continue.

learn from the experts

There is something to learn from all those at the very pinnacle of their sport or profession. In sport it's not just a matter of skill, but how to get the best out of that skill, whether through hard graft or natural flair. In business it's not just a chairman's financial acumen that matters, but the leadership he brings to his profit-making company. Analyse what it is that makes these people so successful and translate those qualities to your own situation.

It's no coincidence that the England Rugby Union team now look closely at other sports, notably Rugby League – once unmentionable where the 15-man game was concerned – and American football for ideas they can develop. Phil Larder, the England team's defensive coach, was actually once in charge of the England Rugby League World Cup team. He has spent considerable time in the USA, studying their particular brand of football. So too has Dave Alred, the kicking coach, who has worked with the Minnesota Vikings.

Many of our top football managers, including Steve McClaren, the Middlesbrough manager and assistant to England coach Sven-Goran Eriksson, also swear by the philosophies formulated by such American sporting luminaries as Vince Lombardi, who, amongst his many achievements, coached the Green Bay Packers from professional losers into winners. More than 30 years after his death he is still fondly remembered for such sayings as: 'If winning isn't everything, why do they keep the score?' and 'If you aren't fired with enthusiasm, you'll be fired with enthusiasm.'

learn from the experts

coaches as motivators

Coaching is a subject about which there will always be much debate. There's no such thing as correct training; no hard and fast rule. In my view, nobody will succeed with fixed ideas. After all, if there were a perfect method, everybody would use it. What *is* certain is that top coaches are also inspiring motivators. This section looks at how they achieve their successes and realize their dreams and those of their teams.

Of course, there are still coaches from the 'old school' – those who are employed because they were once good professionals. But that doesn't make them good coaches. There also used to be a view that a coach did not necessarily have to bring success. Football has long been big business, but it wasn't solely about results. As long as a team stayed in the Premiership, the supporters were happy. To have a team that was winning each week was the ideal. But if you didn't produce the results, then at least if you had a Glenn Hoddle as manager (who was an icon when a player) you had 'bragging rights' over your opponents. Fans of such teams could wallow in the fond belief that they were at least watching football 'as it should be played'.

Over the last few years, though, we have seen the introduction of individuals who have not necessarily boasted a brilliant footballing pedigree, but have become top-class coaches. They have excellent CVs, based primarily on results, and are paid handsomely for their expertise. Look, for example, at the respect given to men such as Sven-Goran Eriksson and Arsène Wenger, neither of whom were gifted players. The attitude towards coaching is changing for the better. Coaches now have a wider sense of how to succeed – and how to inspire their teams to succeed.

Sven-Goran Eriksson is looked upon as one of the world's leading coaches (despite that World Cup defeat by Brazil). His results in competitive matches, despite all the criticism he has received while in charge of England, have been excellent. Essentially, that is what coaching is all about.

The motto for all sports could be the one that's displayed on a board at Twickenham, home of English Rugby Union: 'Winning. That's why we are here.'

TIGER WOODS

As an enthusiastic golfer myself, I have the greatest admiration for Tiger Woods, who's broken through the barriers of achievement and taken his sport to a different level. Recently, however, by his own extraordinary standards, he has had rather a barren period. At the time of writing, he hasn't won a major tournament for some time, but that was inevitable. Less familiar names began to win tournaments, as they enhanced their own games with dedication, practice and help from top coaches and sports psychologists. Talent was emerging all around Tiger, and players raised their game to compete with him. They, like the rest of us, might have admired the man, but they weren't going to sit around accepting that he was the master of all the greens he surveyed and do nothing about it.

Of course anyone, not just top sportsmen, can face defeat at times. Business people are made redundant, a much-desired project goes to the wall, a house sale falls through…but don't let that deter you from trying again, from picking yourself up and starting over. Redefine your goals, decide what is possible, then take things one step at a time and continue along the trail for gold.

Tiger became the inspiration for many young golfers by achieving what he did when still at a relatively young age. Initially, many regarded him with awe. Yet ironically, the long-term effect was to motivate those of his contemporaries with latent ability. Tiger was never going to win everything – not in today's sporting environment, in which top-class coaching, sports scientists and gurus can transform a player.

Tiger is still held in great esteem, despite the dip in his performances. Wherever he plays, he is the crowd-puller. The story of how he ascended to the top of world golf, convincing some people that he was invincible, is a remarkable one. The crowds love to watch him even in defeat because he has risen from winner to legend. He is still thought of as the world's best player, even if his results don't confirm that.

the psychological approach

The strengths of Sir Clive Woodward, coach of England's rugby World Cup-winning team, lie in his ability to look at things in a different way. From what everybody says who worked with him, Clive succeeded because he made sure that he got the best personnel available to do certain jobs. He recognized that no one person can be brilliant at everything, so he employed specialists in defence tactics and kicking, as well as dietitians and fitness trainers, and used up-to-the-minute technology in every way possible. He tried to push back the boundaries of science and technology within sport. His is the stepping-stone approach described in Chapter 4. By dealing with potential problems separately, the goal – in this case, the World Cup win – is achieved.

Clive understands psychology – how to have a mental edge over competitors (see Chapter 8). The Rugby Football Union is relatively well off, so he used its resources to irritate the Australians in the build-up to the 2002 World Cup: the England squad travelled first class, stayed in top-flight accommodation and had the best technical assistance that money could buy. Nothing was too good for Clive's team – and not because he was in a benevolent mood! To those watching from outside, particularly England's rivals, the manner of their travel and treatment represented rewards for success. At that rate, they had to be unbeatable!

As England coach, Clive excelled at looking at the overall picture; not just the technical play on the pitch. His talents included meticulous planning, delegation to the right people, and ensuring that on a particular day his players were in the right shape mentally and physically. On the occasions when the team wasn't as successful as it could have been he would always say in interviews afterwards: 'Well, this is just a stepping-stone. We may have got things wrong

> ## PSYCHOLOGY AT TWICKENHAM
>
> The psychological approach is evident at Twickenham. The changing rooms there are fantastic – if you are a home player. Each man has his own personal area, and once a player is on the squad, he has his nameplate screwed to the wall. The opposition's changing room, on the other hand, is relatively spartan. It consists of benches and whitewashed walls – nothing special.
>
> The home changing rooms help to create an atmosphere of success and quality in every area, a marked contrast to the opposition's.

today, with the opposition playing above themselves, but we've learnt from that, and are moving on.'

It's significant that Arsène Wenger, one of the best football club managers in England, has a similar approach. He studies videos of opponents for hour after hour, he prepares in minute detail, insists on precisely the correct diet for his players, and looks closely at every aspect of recovery training. Unlike 'old school' managers, who tended to tolerate drinking and gambling for the good of team bonding, Arsène does not allow his athletes to go out and do what they shouldn't be doing. He sets specific goals, and plans ahead to achieve them.

parent power

For most young people, their mentors – the people who motivate them – are their parents. That's inevitable in life. But a point of caution: parents themselves should beware of becoming too involved, too pushy, however well-meaning they intend to be. There's a stark difference between support and domination.

If youngsters set out to try and please their parents, they're not setting their own goals and structuring their lives for the right reasons. Remember: it is up to you to decide what you want to achieve and then plan for success. No one else can do this for you.

Fortunately, my parents were supportive without being interfering. There are other good examples. Cyclist Chris Hoy, winner of the 1-km time trial Olympic gold medal at the velodrome in Athens, tells how from the age of seven, when he started riding BMX bikes competitively, his father Dave would drive him to events all over the country and, indeed, abroad. But it was always made clear to young Chris that it was his decision to compete. Hoy senior was in no way attempting to live his life vicariously through his son.

Talent has to be nurtured, not forced out by parental domination.

Redgrave's reminders

- ✔ Success almost certainly doesn't just happen.
- ✔ Expert knowledge is a crucial part of your armoury.
- ✔ Beware – the old ways aren't necessarily the best.
- ✔ Be prepared to learn, and not necessarily from those closest to you.
- ✔ Always listen attentively to the best coaches and bosses: they can help you to raise your standards.

CHAPTER 8

establish a mental edge

REDGRAVE'S RULE:

YOUR MIND CAN BE YOUR GREATEST ASSET.

Your state of mind can often be the decisive factor in whether you will be a winner or loser. Sportsmen and women in particular are guilty of concentrating on their physical prowess at the expense of their mental fitness. In many other areas of life too it is easy to focus on one aspect of a challenge at the expense of the bigger picture.

There are times when you will have to break through the pain barrier – and it won't always be physical pain you have to conquer. Sometimes it's just boredom or fatigue. But whether it's a physical or mental barrier, you'll almost certainly have to face up to it at some stage.

Let's start by looking at what this can mean physically. Maybe you've done a bit of sport, but not for a few years. You feel you want to get fit and lose some weight. The answer is to go out and do some running. You start off and think, 'Hmm, this is quite easy,' but sooner or later, depending on your condition, you'll start to struggle. Nevertheless, you make it back and feel pretty good about yourself. The next day, or soon after, your muscles will start to stiffen. Yes, we've all done it.

What happens is that the lactic acid produced during exercise makes the muscles sore and stiff. The pain is the lactate build-up, and it's probably telling you that you've done too much. You shouldn't have got to that stage in the first place, but it happens to us all. If I go out running, I'll be extremely stiff the next day. What you should do is change to exercise that is less intensive, but do it for a longer period of time, gradually increasing your distance. It's also important to warm up and wind down – first to get the blood flowing before training sessions, and finally to help with recovery. Doing this increases the oxygen in the blood, disperses the lactate and helps get rid of the stiffness within the muscles.

That's the scientific side of it; the reality is that within all forms of training I believe you have to push through the pain barrier in order to recover. Recovery is the important side of training. In other words, the speed with which you recover after exercise is the best indicator of how fit you are.

build up to breakthrough

I remember racing at Henley in 2001. Having retired from competitive rowing by then, I had not done very much training – simply half-hour sessions at low intensity on a rowing machine (what we call steady-state sessions). My aim was to try to hold the split times (the times for each stage) that I used to do in the build-up to Sydney only the year before. I should have been able to do that easily, but when I began my heart rate went through the roof, and it really hurt me to last the whole half-hour. The next session was even worse. The session after that was worse again, and I was thinking: 'Why am I doing this? Why do I want to race at Henley? This is such hard work. I'm not going to get my condition back.' But the fourth session was a vast improvement; it was just a question of conditioning the body.

This steady-state technique can be related to business and the workplace, but in those contexts it is more a question of conditioning your mind. If you've a set amount of work to do, you sometimes think: 'How the hell am I going to get through all this?' There is so much of it that you just keep putting it off, when it's actually far better to get stuck in. Start off slowly, one task at a time, and you will eventually get through the lot.

Of course, timing is an important element. They probably won't thank me for mentioning it, but my daughters' approach to homework is a good example of this. Natalie gets on with it, but Sophie just keeps putting it off until the weekend, partly because she's been working hard at school. There's always some reason for not doing it, so she ends up completing it on Sunday night, but she does it so much better on days when she comes home and simply gets on with it. Similarly, anyone studying for exams will know that they're better off doing revision little and often rather than trying to cram everything at the last moment. People say, 'I'll be all right. I'll crash-revise in the last couple of days.' But the information just doesn't stick. When you're faced with a daunting task, break it down mentally into manageable amounts and you'll be surprised at how much easier it becomes.

The hard work element in business can vary, but it's getting the nitty-gritty done – the equivalent of training – that leads to the big pay-off day. In the workplace, as in sport, you have to complete the basic tasks, the stuff you'd really rather leave because it's boring. It all goes back to what I said about the importance of routine (see pages 121-3). That's why business and sport have a lot in common, especially when it comes to trying to get to the top and then staying there.

be positive rather than negative

This is a crucial area. If you don't deal with negative thoughts and experiences, they can seriously diminish what you achieve. Things will get tough, however well you have planned and structured things, and it's easier to sit down and feel sorry for yourself than it is to carry on.

I was faced with that situation when I came down with colitis (serious inflammation of the colon) only ten weeks before the Barcelona Games in 1992. I could have very easily not done the training, or reduced it significantly during that period. In one sense, I might have felt better, just as anyone would when they're ill. I could have taken three weeks off and concentrated on getting the right treatment to ensure I got the colitis under control.

If the Games had been 18 months away, it might have made sense to have three weeks off. With only ten weeks to go, the options were stark: continue training or miss the Games. I decided to carry on training, and once I was receiving the correct treatment my health started to improve quite quickly. Without the conditioning of rowing up and down the river every day, working on the ergo (rowing machine) and doing weights, my body's essential fitness and stamina wouldn't have been there. Although the quality of my training performance wasn't high, it can be argued that I actually came out stronger. Each training session was just so hard to complete that it built me up.

This doesn't mean – and I must stress this – that whatever is wrong with you, you just work on regardless. Both my conditions, colitis and diabetes, allowed me to continue training. You must be sensible about your particular circumstances and seek medical advice, as I did, otherwise you could damage yourself. In this way, what seems to be a negative in business life – say, an advertising agency losing an important client – can be transformed into a positive if the agency bosses have the get up and go to win another, even more prestigious client straight away.

emerging from dark days

Although I overcame my illness, I had some very dark periods while doing so. The hardest time was when I was at a training camp near Cape Town in late 1997, just after I'd been diagnosed with diabetes. It was a land-based camp and this meant that most of the work was on weights, rowing machines and road cycles. It was torture. After watching me later in the BBC's video diary series *Gold Fever*, James Cracknell commented, 'I never realized you were that ill,' because I was still training, still performing. He and the others had seen me struggle and sometimes fail. I wasn't trying to disguise it, but it was *my* battle. I had to deal with that and get through it.

In circumstances like this you have to look for the light at the end of the tunnel, even if it is only a distant pinprick, and slowly work towards it. From my perspective back in 1997, that light was nearly three years ahead, a glow emanating from Penrith Lakes, location of the 2000 rowing regatta at Sydney. At that point the tunnel for me was extremely long, and the glimmer of light extremely dim.

This example of coping with dark times is an extreme one. We have already discussed how it is essential that you are fit and healthy before attempting to realize your goals. The first thing Jurgen Grobler asked when we discussed my illness with the medical experts was: 'If Steve carries on training, is he damaging his health long term?' If I had been advised by medical opinion to quit that training camp, I'd have agreed, even though I would have found it extremely difficult to accept that decision. What else could I have done? I'm stubborn, but I'm not stupid. You can accept decisions like that if you trust the wisdom of the people you consult.

adjust if you have to

The here and now is important. If you've structured your plan, and you're reassessing and adapting things as you go along, it's easy to say: 'Things aren't going very well at the moment. I'll hold back. I'll just look in a different direction.' In some circumstances, that's a possibility. There is no point in pressing on relentlessly when all the evidence suggests that is the wrong option. If, for example, you plan to run a marathon, but are finding the training really tough, there might be a case for standing still for a while and taking stock. If you are planning to enlarge your company but the sales take a dip, it might be sensible to wait another year to be sure your turnover is high enough. If you're selling your house but the one you want to buy has been bought by someone else, it could be worthwhile putting things on hold until you find another one. Don't always be in a rush. Ask yourself relevant questions:

- Am I really suited to running the marathon? Do I really have the commitment?
- Do I really need to enlarge my company? Would my profits be higher if it stayed the same size?
- Do I really want to sell my house? Will I find another one I like as much?

Sometimes what will be necessary is an adjustment to your strategy or routine. But facing up to a daunting problem can also test your character and determination. The mere fact of being forced to overcome such an adversity could, in the long term, increase your mental strength.

After being diagnosed with diabetes, I had to ask myself a set of questions. If you are in a sport like mine, which is very physical and fitness-related, and you're not feeling well and miss a lot of training, there's only one result: you're going to go backwards. I had to make

establish a mental edge

my own assessment: 'Am I well enough to train? Am I going to get enough out of it if I continue to move forward? Or should I be resting?' Life is always throwing up questions, but sometimes you can't answer them yourself. You need objective advice.

While trying to deal with my diabetes and related issues, the furthest thing from my mind was standing on the rostrum at the Olympic Games and having a gold medal placed around my neck. My immediate concern was all-consuming. I was with a group of guys and wasn't performing very well, but I wasn't going to quit halfway through a training session, even though I felt I should. By the end of each one I had no energy, nothing left to give, but self-pride pushed me on. It became a personal challenge to get through each session.

break down the challenge

How did I cope? I'd simply say to myself: 'Right, I'm going to do one more stroke, and then I'll stop.' And I'd do that stroke and think: 'I've done that one. I can do one more.' I just did it in extremely small increments. If you think about it, my thinking was rather similar to the approach of John Naber, the American swimmer (see page 60).

No matter how hard a task is, the smaller the elements you can break it into, the easier it is to accomplish. Before those training sessions I couldn't have said: 'Right, now I'm going to row 6000 strokes.' Psychologically, it would have destroyed me. That would have been just too hard. However, I always knew I could do one more stroke. It was like asking myself a question every two seconds. 'Can I do this one stroke?' And the answer kept coming: 'Yes, I can.'

When I'd finished the session, even though my performance was poor and not very competitive with the rest of the group, I felt a satisfaction at having completed the task I'd set myself. After that I thought: 'That was really tough, but I got through it. Why can't I tackle the next session?' And I'd get on the road bike the following morning and do it. But had I thought: 'I've got 18 days, and two, three, sometimes four sessions a day.' There's no way I would have coped.

The ultimate goal – the Olympics – was still there, but my illness made it feel further and further away. In the back of my mind I knew that I had to do those training sessions to be at the right level to enable me to compete. Without them there was no way I'd have the chance to achieve that ultimate goal. In this, and other daunting circumstances, you just have to keep reminding yourself: 'You've got to go through the bad times to appreciate the good.'

The irony was that this difficult time actually improved me as an athlete. The challenge of getting through the first couple of years after being diagnosed with diabetes had the effect of strengthening me, both physically and mentally. Grinding through the training, which was as much a battle within my mind as within my body, paid off in the end.

establish a mental edge

> **EXERCISE:** ANALYSE YOUR WAY TO SUCCESS
>
> - Draw up a list of areas you have succeeded in, and those you haven't.
> - Write next to each item why you did or didn't achieve it.
> - Now analyse those reasons more closely. Remember that, as a rule, we all tend to be more negative than positive, finding reasons why we can't do things. People usually say: 'I don't have the time', or 'I've got other commitments', or perhaps 'I don't have enough money'. Try to be constructive rather than destructive.
> - Work backwards to the point you had your dream. Think: 'Do I need to reassess myself? Should I adapt my approach to that goal? Am I totally committed towards what I set out to do?'

It is inevitable that you will question your motivation at some stage during your progress towards your goal. That's why you must have a passion for what you're setting out to do. No half-measures. No thinking, 'Well, I'll just see how it goes.' To achieve anything, you've got to have a major commitment towards it. You won't succeed just by reading this book and writing a few lists. These are only tools along the way, but I hope they will act as catalysts in helping you to create a better life.

lower your rival's expectations

During the course of my rowing career, I learnt many lessons. One was particularly pertinent. Matthew Pinsent and I used to talk, not just about planning to win an event, but about conditioning the opposition to lose, to instil a belief in them that they had no hope of defeating us. Let me explain how we went about this.

In an Olympic final, each boat has a master-plan about how they're going to win. In the next six and half minutes there'll come a realization that it's not going to happen for most of them, but all will have their plan. Sometimes the crew that accepts they'll come last will just go all out, give it their best shot, give absolutely everything from the start line, and hope they can achieve the unexpected. But others in that position will think differently. Perhaps they analyse the race, work out that one of their rivals might try to take on Redgrave and Pinsent, get a couple of lengths' lead by halfway, but then start to struggle and blow up. They would be saying to themselves: 'We could come fifth in an Olympic final! That would be fantastic – far better than our initial expectations.'

That's the way competitors' thinking goes, whether in rowing or any other sport. When we prepared for a final we were very much aware of that. We had a good idea of how our various rivals would approach the race. Some, we knew, would accept that they had no chance of defeating us, and would be rowing for a silver or bronze. What we had to watch out for, as I've stressed before, was the unexpected.

establish a mental edge

Another way to look at it involves using a horse-racing analogy. A jockey who knows that his horse possesses stamina but not much speed will set the pace and stretch his or her opponents whose stamina is suspect. He will utilize his assets fully to the detriment of his rivals. The jockey and trainer will know that there are at least two other horses in the field that are better quality, but if one or both of those fail to respond, their own horse could be runner-up, or maybe win. If, on the other hand, their horse takes on its rivals for speed, it will probably be a hopeless cause.

making use of psychology

Approaching the Barcelona Olympics in 1992, we were beaten by Slovenia in the second regatta of the season. It was a rare defeat for Matthew and me. Slovenia were subsequently beaten at Lucerne by the German crew. We didn't race Slovenia again that season – until the Olympics. Slovenia believed that because they'd beaten us once, they'd beat us again. So, for that matter, did the Germans.

We'd shown no form at all that year, but by the time of the Olympics we felt we were back to our best, although we didn't really know that for certain. We were hoping that we'd draw some strong rivals in our heats so that we could test ourselves. We drew Slovenia. It was the perfect draw for us.

Although they thought they'd beat us, we rowed away from them and cruised to the line, very much in control. We won by three-quarters of a length.

It was an unexceptional race in many ways, but I was tingling with excitement. It was a far better feeling than winning even the final because I knew by then that we were going to win – I was absolutely certain of it. We were back on form and nobody could beat us.

The Slovenian pair crossed the line after us, and as they did so, their heads just dropped. They knew then, even with five days to go, that their chances of winning a gold medal had been cruelly withdrawn.

We drew them and the Germans in the semi-final, and we defeated both of them, but beforehand we were thinking: 'Well, both those crews are relatively young. Is one of them going to come out gunning for us?' We were trying to predict their response, and thought one of them would probably try to lead us.

It didn't happen. With 250 metres (275 yards) gone, I knew we had it won. We just moved away and kept extending our lead. After that, they weren't interested in us. Of course, they were hoping that we'd get something wrong and they might spring a surprise, but basically the Slovenians and Germans were racing each other. The best result they could get was silver.

This is a good example of conditioning a rival to lose. It sounds harsh, even cruel, but at that level of sport the mental side plays a crucial part. Psychologically, we had mastered them in the heat.

The same principle applies in the workplace, where image is vitally important. If you can create an impression that your product is better quality and value than that of your rivals (without actually being negative about them), and thus convince the public that it

establish a mental edge

is more desirable, half your job is done. Your rivals will be bound to think: 'We can't possibly compete with that.' The success of Richard Branson's Virgin empire owes a great deal to the positive image he created.

make it look easy

While you want to beat your rivals, I would like to add a word of caution. It's unnecessary always to inflict a heavy defeat, and counterproductive if it means allowing your opponents to know that you've reached the bottom of your reserves. Appearances can be crucial. Try to appear relaxed.

At one time we thought it was important to win every race by a long distance. The trouble with that is that if you don't, you tend to get disappointed, which isn't good psychology. Eventually, we realized that the margin of victory wasn't especially important: a win was a win. We accepted each victory by whatever margin and analysed it on its own merits. We took the positives or negatives from it and worked through to the next race.

This approach was something that James Cracknell struggled with when we formed the coxless four, with Sydney as our target. We might have been capable of winning a race by three or four seconds more than we did, and he got frustrated because we didn't. I used to say to him: 'One day you'll be in a situation where you have to dig really deep to be able to come through because it won't happen the way you planned it. If you're digging deep every time you race, and you're putting in your best performance when you've got the ability to win anyway, you're letting everybody else know exactly how much you've got in reserve, and they can train to beat that. It's better that they're not quite sure how much you've got in hand.'

However you finish a race – hard, easy or in between – you're trying to make it look as though it didn't hurt. Sometimes it did, sometimes it didn't. But however deep you have to dig into your mental and physical stamina, you don't want to show your opponents that they actually gave you a tough race. In fact, the tougher the race, the more relaxed you should try to be. It's similar to a batsman being struck painfully by a ball from a fast bowler. If he doesn't show he's hurt or injured, it's a psychological boost, conditioning his opponent to believe that he can't be damaged, while strengthening faith in his own prowess. This approach also works in other walks of life. In business, for example, it's a double whammy if you win a competitive bid, then give the impression to your rivals that you achieved your success almost effortlessly. They might think twice about competing with you again.

persevere and believe in yourself

When everything appears to be going against you, that is the time for perseverance and self-belief – the time to look back at the goals you set yourself at the start, the plan of action you decided on and the strategy you planned over a long period.

establish a mental edge

The French rowing pair at Barcelona in 1992 finished fifth in the final, and regarded it as a good result. Four years later at Atlanta they won a bronze. That was a fine result for them. After that they were beaten by different crews in nearly every race until they finally won the world championship in 1997 in their own country. By that time, Matthew and I had moved on to the coxless four, while the powerful Australians had taken a year out. The French then won a silver medal in the 1999 world championships, being beaten by the Aussie pair. Finally, a year later, they claimed the Olympic gold. Their reward shows you that perseverance can pay dividends. They were determined to live their dream, and succeeded by having patience and fortitude.

THE VITAL MENTAL EDGE

I was always fascinated by what the athlete Daley Thompson had to say about his success. I always suspected that he employed similar mental preparation to me. Just as I stumbled into rowing by accident, Daley 'fell' into his own sport, the decathlon. He was an excellent sprinter, although not the best, and like myself, he defeated athletes blessed with more natural gifts.

This was because Daley did not leave his career in the hands of luck or hope. He assumed that he would excel until it was proven otherwise. For example, Daley famously used to say that he planned to train on Christmas Day. I did, too – for the same reason as Daley: because I knew that our opponents probably wouldn't be. Both of us would be getting a psychological advantage over our rivals.

> In reality, of course, it wouldn't make any difference whether I trained on that day or not. In the great scheme of things, one day wouldn't make all that much difference, but it gave me an inner strength. To my mind, I was getting one over my opposition – even though they weren't aware of it. I built up my own mental strength from it. That's important when you have to dig deep.

beware of mind games

We hear a lot about how sportsmen and women attempt to psych out the opposition. At the top level in football the gamesmanship, or mind games, between Sir Alex Ferguson and Arsène Wenger are legendary. Each attempts to gain a psychological advantage by creating doubt in his rival's mind before matches between them.

Craig Mahoney, professor of applied sports psychology at Wolverhampton University, who advises our top referees on handling stress and pressures, says: 'Gamesmanship is normally between players, but it can also be between a manager and a referee, or a manager and the media. We're all influenced by what others say. A lot of comments are not designed to have an immediate impact, but for the recipient to go away and have it fester in their mind to the point where it can screw them up.

'The more experienced a manager, the more likely he is to try and gain an advantage. Sir Alex Ferguson is pretty astute at making comments that he knows will resonate around the minds of other people, particularly other managers.'

Gamesmanship between players, on the other hand, tends to take place on the field. It can range from winning decisions by pretending to have been fouled, to constant badgering of the referee in an attempt to win his favour.

Wherever it occurs, 'winding up' the opposition can often have the opposite effect to that desired. We've all heard of the football manager who, when his team have been condemned or belittled in the media by a counterpart whose side they are about to play, pastes cuttings of those comments above each player's dressing-room peg. As they say, 'He's done his team talk for him.'

Football is not alone in using mind games. Top-class cricket is as much a mental game as a physical one, particularly when fielders indulge in 'sledging' (verbally abusing) a batsman at the crease in an attempt to undermine him. Indeed, in virtually every high-profile sport words reported by the media or spoken out on the field of play are an attempt to chip away at a rival's confidence and cast self-doubt.

Matthew and I had a policy of not winding up our opposition, which James, for one, found difficult because of his enthusiasm for the battle. We also tended not to be overfriendly with other crews. We always chatted to people if they chatted to us because if we upset them, what would they do? They would become even more determined to beat us. This might sound cynical, but the friendlier you are with people, the less determined they are to try and beat you.

Beware of using these techniques without thinking them through carefully. Some can work for you, but others can do the opposite. Many are the occasions when a footballer, for example, has cast aspersions on the opposing team's prowess, only to have the insult backfire and make the opposition even more intent on winning.

It is important that you play mind games to your advantage rather than to your opponents', and that applies in business as much as sport. Promoting your own product at the expense of your rival's may be profitable, but it can also expose you and make you vulnerable to attack. It's rather like politics. Condemning the opposition comes easily to most politicians, and might win them points in the polls. However, it might also draw attention to their own party's past inadequacies and thus rebound on them.

If you are tempted to indulge in mind games, use visualization first to think through the possible effects (see page 102). They may not be quite what you intend.

Redgrave's reminders

✔ Work your way through the bad times: it will help you to appreciate the good ones.
✔ Be positive when a problem crops up.
✔ If a challenge is daunting, approach it step by step.
✔ Use psychology to stay ahead, but...
✔ ...beware of mind games – you could be the loser.

CHAPTER 9

leadership and working within a team

> REDGRAVE'S RULE:
>
> *A GOOD TEAM PLAYER IS SOMEONE WHO ADDS TO THE ENVIRONMENT THEY'RE IN.*

This book is aimed at individuals, but it is highly unlikely that you will achieve your goals without the aid of others. When I was preparing for the Sydney Olympics, it was very similar to being a key employee in a small company. Our team of four did exactly the same type of work, though with subtly different skills and strengths, and had a very close involvement with each other, aiming towards a particular achievement. In the workplace it might have been a sales target. For us it was a race.

As I say in the talks I give, it's essential to consider the make-up of the team and the responsibilities of each member. A team is not just a group of people with similar abilities. It's much more than that. There has to be a chemistry that allows you to complement each other, even if you're not compatible. A team also has to be well led. I was always thought of as the 'leader' of the boats I rowed in, but that was just how it appeared because I was the oldest and most experienced. I don't think that should necessarily make you the leader.

Even back in 1984, that first Olympic gold-winning crew was known as the 'Redgrave Four', despite the fact that another member, Martin Cross, had at that stage achieved more than me. This probably came about because I had already developed a name with my single sculling exploits.

Interestingly, many good leaders are reluctant to take on the job – it is never an easy one – and I certainly never thought of myself as a leader. I was always uncomfortable being thought of as that, although obviously my experience would be an asset. In rowing you have a coach, and within the boat everybody has an individual role. You all have to blend in and perform to the best of your ability in order to be successful. Any business is the same: there is someone who leads, and the team works together with the leader to achieve the company's objectives.

leadership qualities

Within your team, you're a leader, a good one, a strong character, single-minded. Everyone says so, but have you listened to what your team is saying to you? If you're part of a group, you have to be able to listen to people. It's not a sign of weakness. Feedback from the team must be taken into account. There can't be a dictatorship; there must be give and take. You can bet your life that even those who are reputedly autocrats, such as Rupert Murdoch, may appear to be tyrannical, but actually spend a lot of time listening to those working for them. Even if you're the boss, you can still learn from those you have working for you.

As a member of a team, you have to believe in what you're doing. If you're a dictator, demanding that something be done a certain way because there's only one way of doing it, you won't get the best out of your team unless they believe in the same strategy as you. Their hearts are not going to be in it.

WHAT MAKES A GOOD LEADER?

To be a good leader, you need to:
- Enthuse everyone involved so that they feel part of the team and confident in what they're doing. This element alone is crucial to success.
- Know when to be firm and exude authority, when to listen, and when to accept change.
- Look for improvement – constantly. You can be successful for one day, even for one year, but the chances are that the opposition have watched what you've done, have learnt from it, copied and adapted it, and tried to improve upon it.
- Constantly seek new ideas and break new ground. If you're top of whatever field you're in, there are no guidelines for staying there. It often comes down to trial and error.
- Identify targets. In a sports team targets are simple to identify: the Olympics, world championships, and so on. Within the workplace, it's different. Some people look out for themselves rather than the company, especially in large corporations.
- Enhance performances by improving the concentration of employees. This can be done by offering incentive schemes, such as bonuses or share options.
- Implement technical improvements, such as updated computer systems, that will make your company more efficient.

The problem in the workplace is that while you're improving your own status within a company, it may be detrimental to the team you're working with. That's where middle and higher management come into the picture, blending the unit together. This might require tough decisions, particularly when handing out promotion. Those who have been there longest may be not right for the job.

A leader's role is very much like a coach's. In our case Jurgen's role was to marshal the training and schedules. He watched nearly every training session we did – in the gym, on the water – just being there, always looking at small details and relating them to the bigger picture, ensuring that everything was going to plan. In some respects, we saw him as an outsider. There was ribbing between ourselves and Jurgen about us doing the work while he simply set it up. But if somebody else dared criticize him, we'd be united behind him. I bet the same is true of Sir Alex Ferguson. No doubt the players curse him at times when they're training, but in public they'd back him to the hilt. That's human nature.

LEADERSHIP FROM THE TOP

Barbara Cassani headed up the London 2012 Olympic bid from the time it was launched until May 2004, when the capital reached the shortlist, and she has remained its deputy chair. Barbara, who first made her name as the highly successful chief executive of the no-frills airline Go, once told me: 'I'm no good at coming up with ideas. But I know lots of people who can, and I'm quite happy to go and pinch those ideas and structure them in a way that they will be successful. All I can do is organize.'

All she can do?

The ability to organize, to administrate, to create a structure in which people operate successfully is a great talent. However, the crucial thing her comments reveal is that she is quite aware of her strengths and weaknesses. She has vision and energy. In her job with the airline she would have delegated others to work on novel ideas for increasing ticket sales. She would have concentrated on pulling the whole thing together.

Her dream, if you like, was to create a successful airline, but she was realistic enough to know that she couldn't do it unless she recruited the most talented people around in their particular spheres.

teamwork – the secret of success

It might be stating the obvious, but teamwork is crucial to success. It is important that everyone within a team feels comfortable and is given an opportunity to contribute. In both business and sport, nobody, not even the chairman or coach, stops learning. The 'Redgrave Four' developed a strong relationship with Mike Spracklen and Jurgen Grobler in which we learnt together and looked at ideas that people had never used before in the UK. It wasn't just a case of them laying down rules. We worked as a team.

Teamwork is not necessarily about suppressing your own ego. You've still got to be yourself. Being forthright does not come naturally to me, but if I think something's not right, I'll say so. Similarly, if your character is to be a bit more outgoing, you shouldn't hold that back. A good team has a sharing environment. A good team player is someone who can add to the environment they're in, being able to cope with criticism and contribute ideas, while accepting that they might not be taken up.

In my sport, you could assemble the best four rowers in the world, but that wouldn't necessarily make them the fastest four because they'd each have their own ways of achieving things. Potentially, of course, they should be the best in the world. Like a racing car, if they've got the right components and are fine-tuned, they'll win; if not, they can rise to a certain level, but probably won't be able to go all the way. A winning team is about working with the right assets. In my sport it was always a case of starting off with raw elements and blending them together over a period of time to ensure long-term success.

When Matthew Pinsent, James Cracknell, Tim Foster and I were put together as a four, it would have been logical to put the two biggest, strongest guys in the middle, and the more dynamic guys at either end. In theory, Matthew and I should have been in the middle. We tried all sorts of combinations until we arrived at the formation we finally kept, and we got there by trial and error. We had the best athletes in the country, but we still had to experiment before becoming the world's best.

As with any team in any walk of life, we had to rely on each other, particularly if somebody was ill. People would say was there a concern about my diabetes. Well, yes, I'm sure there was, but the others relied on me to get it under control and do what was right to get the performance I needed. It's pointless worrying about somebody else's health or injury. You have to get on with what you're doing. If one person was out, the rest of us would carry on as normal. It's sometimes hard to do that, but that's what any team has to do. It's easier for an individual to catch up on fitness and reach the point that the unit has moved on to than for everyone to come to a halt, twiddle their thumbs, then try to move on from where they all left off.

A team has to be bigger than that.

OUR WINNING TEAM

Matthew Pinsent, as the stroke of the boat, established the rhythm and pace. He was the shop-steward, if you like. We could always enhance what he was doing, but we couldn't take his role away from him. We had to follow what he demanded.

Tim Foster was not as strong an athlete as the rest of us on rowing machines and physical tests, but he was very good at the technical side. This compensated for his weaker areas, so he ran all the technical sessions, in which we endeavoured to hone our technique in order to get the optimum power from the boat.

James Cracknell used to run the work sessions, and was basically 'Mr Motivator', running the day-to-day grind of work within the boat.

My role as leader was to bring my experience to bear. Having had more races than everyone else, I was like a tactician, in charge of the race situation. When racing, I also did all the 'calls' (demanding the number of strokes required a minute and deciding when to push on), but James did them in training. Another of my roles was to steer the boat (yes, it does need doing!) with my foot in a pivoted steering shoe connected to rudder lines along the sides.

We were all doing the same stroke, levering our body weight on the oars simultaneously, pushing the blades through the water at the same time, but we all had those slightly different roles, which most people don't realize. It worked well for us.

chemistry is crucial

The fastest crew doesn't necessarily come from putting the best athletes together. The chemistry between the members of the crew is also crucial. Andy Holmes, my first Olympic partner, and I had very different backgrounds. We never socialized, but we were very successful in what we did. Matthew and I had the same desire, but we got on together as well and enjoyed doing other things together, such as playing golf.

It's said that a happy crew is a slow crew, never row with your best friends, but I've never believed that. I remember a four (from the 1980 Olympics) that included Martin Cross, who now, among his other interests, analyses rowing events for BBC Radio 5-Live. As a crew, their results outshone their ability because they all believed in each other and their coach. Their grit and determination achieved them very good results.

The important aspect of teamwork is that, regardless of your relationships, you have a single-minded sense of purpose about what you want to achieve. People point out, even now, how competitive Matthew Pinsent and I were with each other. Whether playing cards, rowing, or on the ergo in the gym, we wanted to beat each other. As long as that competition remains healthy, that's a good thing.

a team is a support structure

I always used to believe that if you had talent, it would be enhanced if you had a good coach, but that excellence would come out whatever the situation. It wasn't until I started to suffer from colitis and diabetes that I realized just how many people at the fringes made a difference to the smooth running of our team.

Jurgen was in that category. He was there with us all the time. When we stood on the rostrum at Sydney to receive our gold medals there should have been one for him too. In some ways he was part of the unit; in others he was slightly distant. Yet he was always the mainstay of the structure: the central pole of the big top. It would have collapsed without him.

There were others as well. Think of the unit as a giant road bridge crossing a river. When you approach it, all you see is the tarmac. That represents us, the crew; the guys people watch on TV – the visual manifestation of the whole project. The strength of that structure lies in the foundations underneath. The tarmac does nothing to support the structure; it merely ensures a smooth ride. The back-up staff of physios, doctors and masseurs all ensured our fitness and well-being; the team manager and administrative staff organized transport and sorted out the logistics of the operation. Between training sessions we'd take it for granted that food and drink would be available, but that was thanks to the chefs at the Leander Club. We'd achieve what we did regardless, but that back-up did make the whole thing smoother and easier.

That's why it's important that your 'team' – your family, your friends, your employees or team-mates – supports you as you aim for your goal. If you are a leader, that's why it's important to take the people around you into your confidence and allow them to help you on your way. It's a bit like training as a team – each individual helps, and is helped in return.

have faith in your team

Once you're convinced that your preparation is correct, ensure that the whole team – whether coaches, team-mates, work colleagues or friends – consists of people that you can trust and believe in. That doesn't mean, incidentally, that you have to be friends with them. Indeed, it's possibly preferable not to be if you are seeking an objective view on your progress or performance.

If you are told something that you don't believe 100 per cent – you think the advice is biased – you won't put 100 per cent effort into what you are doing, and you won't get 100 per cent out of it. If you have doubts in your mind about what you're being told, things are likely to fall apart when the pressure is on.

Looking back to the early 1990s, I must admit that if Jurgen had turned up at a different time in my development, such as immediately after an Olympic victory, our relationship might not have worked. As it was, the year before he arrived Matthew and I had crossed the line only third in the Tasmania World Championships, which we were both aware wasn't good enough. We knew we had to buckle down to the training, so it was an opportune moment for Jurgen to arrive. Two years earlier I was in a different mindset: I doubt I'd have had faith in his methods. In all honesty, I don't think we would have hit it off.

> ### COPY AND IMPROVE ON SUCCESS
>
> It's human nature to copy a successful leader, but it's important to extract the reality from the myths. Once you've done that, you can adapt the winning strategies to your own situation and try to improve on their success.
>
> Look closely at how successful leaders train, how they race or how they run their company. Analyse the information and think: 'I could do that, but I'm not just going to copy them. If I could tweak their strategy here or change it there, I could improve on it and make it fit my needs.'

does a leader have to be ruthless?

I'm not a greater believer in ruthlessness. What I do believe is that a leader, whether of a sports team or a business, has to be dedicated and focused on what he or she is doing. I'd call it single-minded determination.

This doesn't mean you have to be cut-throat in your approach, but it does mean that occasionally you have to take hard decisions – ones that will inevitably upset people. This happens when someone is taken out of a crew, or when a member of staff is made redundant.

learn from defeat

We have all probably suffered defeat at some stage in life, whether as athletes, business leaders or private individuals. But it is important to regard defeat positively, as something to be learnt from. This applies especially if you are the leader of a team and need to keep morale high. When England's rugby side lost some games they perhaps should have won early on in his stewardship, Sir Clive Woodward was correct in his claim that you learn more from defeat than you do from success. The former highlights areas for improvement; the latter tends to conceal deficiencies that may become apparent only when the opposition is more daunting. Treat defeat as a useful lesson; be wary of victory.

What happens, though, if defeat is rare? When Matthew Pinsent and I went through a series of races unbeaten, we'd come back from international regattas after winning and say to ourselves: 'We've won that, but we could have done better. We didn't win in the manner we'd like to have done.' The moral of this is: never rest on your laurels. If you have a success, build on it. Add to your list of goals and dreams to be realized, and you're sure to be a winner – whether as a leader, a member of a team or simply as someone who gets the maximum out of life.

Redgrave's reminders

✔ Good teamwork is the secret of success.
✔ Personal chemistry is crucial in a team environment.
✔ You don't have to be close friends to be best team-mates.
✔ Your team is your support structure.
✔ Treat losing as a useful lesson, not an occasion for regret.

CHAPTER 10

enjoying success and facing the future

REDGRAVE'S RULE:

' APPRECIATE THE MOMENT. '

Many people find the journey more enjoyable than arrival at the destination. Setting goals and working towards them may be so absorbing that finally realizing them can be something of an anticlimax – as I can testify from experience. You shouldn't worry if you feel something similar when you've realized your own dream. During my career, each time I achieved my goal of an Olympic gold medal I very quickly focused on the next target. I did not dwell on that particular success, even though for that moment I was a star of the greatest sporting show on Earth.

Of course, winning at life is different. It is about the effect you have on others, the respect you feel for yourself, your sense of achievement, and the knowledge that you are the best you can be. And all this will impact on you every day – not just once in every four years.

In Los Angeles in 1984, after my first gold medal, I was absolutely thrilled and jumping around with joy. Then the next thing I thought was: 'OK, done that. What do I do now?' You, too, might be satisfied with what you've done, but also feel a little bit lost. You may be thinking: 'This is the stepping-stone to other gold medals,' as I did, but that's only in the back of your mind. After Matthew Pinsent and I won our first gold medal together in

enjoying success

Barcelona in 1992, I couldn't think what to do next. For any Olympian, whose whole lifestyle has been focused on that one day for four years, the problem is that you don't look beyond it. However, the moment you cross that final winning line, everything is different – not you as a person, but your immediate focus. It's not just that you don't have to go out training the day after winning: you're simply looking forward to the next challenge.

It was only at Sydney, where I knew I was going to retire after winning that fifth gold, that I could actually sit back and congratulate myself – albeit in a very low-key way: 'That was pretty impressive. How could I get it right five times when there are four years between each one?' I'd never really thought about that before.

I find it very interesting in sport, in which success is obviously very visual, that so many winners cross the line and celebrate exuberantly. I'm inclined to think that they didn't really believe they could win. Those who are more conservative in their celebrations probably did believe they were going to win and that they were only equalling their expectations.

Whichever way you respond to your success, I believe it is important never to forget those who helped get you there, and those you beat to the winning line. In the thrill of success it's not uncommon to overlook the people who have given help and support. I probably wasn't any different at the beginning of my career. I was certainly different by the end.

That's why after our crew had crossed the winning line at Sydney we made a point of paddling past the huge British crowd and thanking them before returning to the landing stage; and why we shook the hands of the other medallists before we spoke to the media. The race was as good as it was because of our rivals, particularly the Italian crew, who were runners-up, and the atmosphere was created by the crowd. It was also time to appreciate our coach Jurgen Grobler and, where I was concerned, his predecessor Mike Spracklen. Together they had contributed significantly towards my successes.

living the life of a legend

I hope my own story will have stimulated you sufficiently to fulfil your own dream and inspire you to seek a new challenge.

But what does a five gold medal-winning Olympian do when he's lived the dream? Do it again? Back in the autumn of 2003, when I was out running one day, I did contemplate making a return and maybe taking part in the Athens Games. That desire to seek a new challenge hadn't been completely quelled by retirement I suppose, and had been stimulated by hearing Matthew Pinsent and James Cracknell talk about switching from a pair to a four, which ultimately they did. Why not join them, I thought? The following day, my muscles stiff after that run, I decided it was maybe not such a good idea after all. But then I got to thinking: 'It's possible. You go to the world championships, and you're seeing people that you used to be able to beat very easily winning medals. Why not?'

Most of the time, good preparation will help you to achieve your goals, but that's not always the case. The human body is quite peculiar in how it gets performances out of itself. While I believe I could have regained a high percentage of my fitness in the year that was left before the Athens Olympics, it might not have been enough. I was then 42, and knew there had been a 41-year-old who won a silver medal in recent years, but I wanted to get back to the personal bests of my own career. Was that possible? I doubted it.

Sometimes I look back and think: 'If I didn't have colitis and diabetes, what kind of performances could I have produced?' If I had my health, I'm sure I could have made a comeback. The thought kept going through my mind: 'How high can I go?' Coincidentally, I had a conversation at that time with Greg Searle, who, together with his brother Jonny, won an Olympic gold medal at Barcelona in 1992 in the coxed pairs. He talked about forming a pair with me, and said: 'You are the one reason I would come out of retirement.'

Were it not for my health problems, I know I could have prepared myself sufficiently well to take part in the Athens Olympics. The structure would have been there, overseen by head coach Jurgen Grobler within the British Rowing Association. Also, I had gained over 25 years' experience since first clambering into a rowing boat, and that alone was enough to bolster my thoughts of achieving what many would have considered the impossible.

It was a dream, of course, but my life has been a series of dreams, and in rowing I have realized all of them. While it's nice to dream, I did not want to taint what I'd already achieved by not succeeding. Also, having already threatened to retire immediately after Atlanta in 1996, I didn't want to end up as rowing's answer to the comeback supremo Frank Sinatra. Remember, I was the

Olympic rower who famously commanded that he should be shot 'if I am ever seen in a boat again'. Four years after that announcement I was receiving a gold medal at Sydney…

Pros and cons batted back and forth within my mind, but the decision had to be no. Life had moved on. If I'd gone ahead, I know people would have said: 'He's crazy. Why do it?' But if you don't try, how do you know? How do you know you cannot attain a higher level? After one Olympic gold I could have said: 'I've done it now. I've achieved the ultimate within our sport. Thanks very much, but I'm off to do something else.' In fact, when pondering whether to try for a sixth gold, realism took hold pretty rapidly. There's no point having dreams that are beyond your capabilities, and the reality was that I knew my medical conditions would make another attempt impossible.

So how much do I still heed the lessons I have preached in this book? I have to be honest. I always said I'd give myself an Olympiad (four years) off after more than 25 years of focus on rowing. That doesn't mean there hasn't been a structure to the things I've been involved with in that time: the London 2012 bid, in which I'm a small cog in a big machine, is a case in point. Then there's my clothing company, Five Gold, a charitable trust. These interests take big chunks of my time, but not in a formal way.

The only area I haven't been tempted to move into is coaching, although I feel I'd actually make a very good coach because of my experience. It was a possibility on my post-retirement list, but I decided it was unrealistic and not right for me. As it is, there haven't been enough hours in the day to do all the things I'd like to be involved in and still have time for my family. Having done one activity extremely well for a long period of time, I'm now doing many things, but almost certainly not to the expert level I'd wish to do them.

I'm now ready to set my goals and structure my life more precisely. And start dreaming again…

As you will do after reading this book, I will identify and define my dreams, estimate whether I have the potential to fulfil them, and plan my strategies for realizing them. I will use my experience as an elite athlete to progress along this new pathway towards my new goals – and, I hope, will again be a winner, but this time in a new stage of my life.

Redgrave's reminders

- ✔ The future begins in the present – allow time to appreciate your accomplishments.
- ✔ Keep striving. Once you have achieved your goal, look forward to the next challenge.
- ✔ Never forget those who helped you to achieve your success.
- ✔ Winning at life is about the effect you have on others, it is about the respect you feel for yourself, your sense of achievement, and the knowledge that you are the best you can be.
- ✔ Believe in your dreams – today's dreams have the power to become your future.

steve redgrave timeline

1962   Born 23 March in Marlow, Buckinghamshire.

1976   Introduced to rowing at Great Marlow School, where he is coached by a teacher, Francis Smith.

Wins first race as a member of a school crew at Avon County Schools Regatta.

1979   First coached by Marlow-based Mike Spracklen, a former top sculler, who was later to coach the Great Britain women's squad, and in 2004 coached the Canadian crew who nearly thwarted the gold medal success of the British coxless four.

1983   First wins Diamond Sculls at Henley Royal Regatta. Would win that event several more times, and the Silver Goblets a record seven times.

1984   Wins first Olympic gold medal at Los Angeles in coxed fours.

1986   Wins three Commonwealth gold medals at Edinburgh in the single scull, coxless pairs and coxed four.

1987   Awarded the MBE in the New Year's Honours List.

1988   Wins Olympic gold at Seoul in the coxless pairs (with Andy Holmes); also wins bronze in the coxed pairs.

1989–90   Becomes a member of the British bobsleigh team.

1990   Matthew Pinsent becomes his new pairs partner.

1991   Former East German coach Jurgen Grobler takes over Great Britain's men's rowing squad.

1992   Wins Olympic gold in the coxless pairs at Barcelona (with Matthew Pinsent); is also flag-bearer for the British Olympic Team at the opening ceremony.

1994   Sets world record time in coxless pairs at Lucerne (with Matthew Pinsent).

1996   Wins Olympic gold in the coxless pairs at Atlanta (with Matthew Pinsent), setting Olympic record time; is again Great Britain's flag-bearer at the opening ceremony. Immediately after race, famously declares: 'If anybody sees me near a boat again, they have my permission to shoot me. I've had enough.' Four months later declares that he intends to carry on to Sydney 2000.

1997   Awarded the CBE in the New Year's Honours List.

1999   Wins his ninth World Championship gold medal at St Catherine's, Canada, having previously won in 1986, 1987, 1991, 1993, 1994, 1995, 1997 and 1998.

2000   Wins Olympic gold in the coxless four, which makes him the only athlete in an endurance event to have won gold medals at five consecutive Olympic Games.

Is voted BBC Sports Personality of the year

2001   Awarded a knighthood in the New Year's Honours List.

Completes London marathon.

2003   Is voted BBC Golden Sports Personality of the last 50 years.

Redgrave's reminders

Identify Your Dreams
Never look back with regret and think of 'what might have been'. To achieve your dreams, you must have a Vision and a Target. Keep reminding yourself that you can achieve your goal, rather than search for reasons why you cannot.

- ✔ Identify your dreams – think as big and bold as you like.
- ✔ Let your mind wander and think the unthinkable. Be adventurous.
- ✔ Take time off to focus on your dreams.
- ✔ Face reality and consider the implications of your dreams.
- ✔ Make your dreams manageable – but don't limit yourself.

What is Your Potential?
You owe it to yourself to fulfil your potential. Learn to evaluate yourself as honestly as possible. Utilize your strengths and improve on your weaker areas.

- ✔ Analyse your strengths and weaknesses – honestly.
- ✔ Decide what motivates you before you embark on your journey.
- ✔ Ask yourself how ambitious you are.
- ✔ Decide whether you are a risk-taker or a percentage player.
- ✔ Be truthful about your abilities. Otherwise you will cheat only one person: yourself.

Plan to Succeed
All you can do is equal your expectations. Make sure that your expectations are high and put steps in place to help you to achieve them. Whatever your ambitions, keep your goals manageable and in sight because they will allow you to measure your progress.

- ✔ Set yourself precise goals.
- ✔ Stretch yourself, but keep your goals manageable and in sight.
- ✔ Break everything down into achievable chunks.
- ✔ Focus on what is possible.
- ✔ Once you have succeeded for the first time, you have proved to yourself that there's no reason why you can't do so again.
- ✔ Set your own gold standards.

Be Flexible and Use Stepping Stones
You've defined your goals and decided on your strategy but don't be deterred if things don't go as planned. Stay flexible; there's always more than one way to

achieve what you have set out to do. Allowing time to pause and reflect may enable you to make a better choice.

- ✔ In the real world things never go smoothly.
- ✔ Nothing is written in stone.
- ✔ Be prepared for the unexpected.
- ✔ Pressure can be good for you – it's a stepping-stone on the way to success.
- ✔ Be aware of your capabilities, and be prepared to adapt them.

Look Ahead and Stay Ahead

The athlete that crosses the finishing line first is the one with the mental edge. Learn to use your mind to increase your winning ability by using visualization techniques for mental rehearsal. Visualization helps mental preparation. Rehearsing different options in your mind will allow you to develop winning tactics.

- ✔ Turn your mind into a mental DVD player.
- ✔ Expect the unexpected to happen.
- ✔ Stay one step ahead – don't be lost for answers.
- ✔ Be prepared to deal with stress.
- ✔ Control what can be controlled.

Train to Win

Some people train to win. I train to eliminate the possibility of defeat. Flair, talent and natural ability are only part of the answer. Winning ability is all about creating consistent performances. To get to the top and remain there you have to maintain a highly focused regime.

- ✔ Hard work is the necessary evil if you want to win at life.
- ✔ Cream doesn't necessarily rise to the top.
- ✔ Learn to love routine, not despise it.
- ✔ Reward yourself when you achieve a training goal – you deserve it.
- ✔ Exercise must be fun.

Learn from the Experts

Don't be afraid to learn and seek inspiration from others. Striving for a goal is like going into battle: expert knowledge is a crucial part of your armoury. Learn not just from other people's successes but also from their mistakes. Success doesn't just happen by itself; you need to know how to optimise your skill.

- ✔ Success almost certainly doesn't just happen.
- ✔ Expert knowledge is a crucial part of your armoury.
- ✔ Beware – the old ways aren't necessarily the best.
- ✔ Be prepared to learn, and not necessarily from those closest to you.
- ✔ Always listen attentively to the best coaches and bosses: they can help you to raise your standards.

Establish a Mental Edge
Your state of mind is a decisive factor in whether you will be a winner or loser. No matter how hard the task, the smaller the elements the task can be broken into, the easier it is to accomplish. Ask yourself 'Can I do just one more?' The answer will usually be: 'Yes, I can.'

- ✔ Work your way through the bad times: it will help you to appreciate the good ones.
- ✔ Be positive when a problem crops up.
- ✔ If a challenge is daunting, approach it step by step.
- ✔ Use psychology to stay ahead, but…
- ✔ …beware of mind games – you could be the loser.

Leadership and Working Within a Team
It is unlikely that you will achieve your goals without the aid of others. A team is not just a group of people with similar abilities; it's much more than that. There needs to be a chemistry that allows you to complement each other's skills, even if you're not compatible.

- ✔ Good teamwork is the secret of success.
- ✔ Personal chemistry is crucial in a team environment.
- ✔ You don't have to be close friends to be best teammates.
- ✔ Your team is your support structure.
- ✔ Treat losing as a useful lesson, not an occasion for regret.

Enjoying Success and Facing the Future
Many people find the journey more enjoyable than arrival at the destination. Setting goals and working towards them may be so absorbing that finally realizing them can be something of an anticlimax. Make time to enjoy the moment; don't just look forward – your life is happening in the present.

- ✔ The future begins in the present – allow time to appreciate your accomplishments.
- ✔ Keep striving. Once you have achieved your goal, look forward to the next challenge.
- ✔ Never forget those who helped you to achieve your success.
- ✔ Winning at life is about the effect you have on others, it is about the respect you feel for yourself, your sense of achievement, and the knowledge that you are the best you can be.
- ✔ Believe in your dreams – today's dreams have the power to become your future.